IGCSE

English as a Second Language

Second edition

Peter Lucantoni

Nicholas Lo

CAMBRIDGE
UNIVERSITY PRESS

CAMBRIDGE UNIVERSITY PRESS
Cambridge, New York, Melbourne, Madrid, Cape Town, Singapore, São Paulo

Cambridge University Press
The Edinburgh Building, Cambridge CB2 2RU, UK

www.cambridge.org
Information on this title: www.cambridge.org/9780521546942

First published 2001
Second edition 2004
4th printing 2006

Printed in Dubai by Oriental Press

A catalogue record for this publication is available from the British Library

ISBN-13 978-0-521-54694-2 paperback
ISBN-10 0-521-54694-X paperback

ACKNOWLEDGEMENTS
Index, design, page layout and artwork illustrations by Hardlines, Charlbury, Oxford

To the three girls in my life: Lydia, Sara and Emily.

Contents

Introduction

This second edition is intended for students who are taking the revised International General Certificate of Secondary Education (IGCSE) in English as a Second Language (E2L) (first exam May/June 2006). It has been completely updated to take into account all the changes in the new syllabus 0510. It is assumed that most of you who use this book will be studying English in order to promote your educational or employment prospects, and it therefore includes topics and themes relevant to these goals. You will find passages and activities based on a wide variety of stimulating subjects, which I hope you will enjoy reading and discussing.

The book is divided into four themed parts: Leisure and entertainment, Work and education, People and relationships, and Ideas and the future. Each themed part is sub-divided into units based on the specific skill areas of the IGCSE E2L examination: reading, writing and listening. There are also four units providing examination practice. Speaking skills are practised through discussion activities and pair and group work, which occur in every unit. At the end of each unit there is a selection of Further practice exercises, so that you can do extra work at home or without a teacher.

The material becomes progressively more demanding, with longer and more advanced texts used in the second half of the book. The first three exam practice units (5, 10 and 15) contain a selection of exercises related to the material covered in the preceding units, whereas exam practice Unit 20 is a complete sample examination paper. This progressive step-by-step approach, including exam tips, will help to build your confidence in all the main skill areas, while also developing the techniques and additional skills necessary for success in the IGCSE E2L examination.

This book covers both the Core and Extended curriculums of the syllabus. Where applicable, marks are shown for Core and Extended questions. E is used to differentiate Extended curriculum questions from Core curriculum questions, unless stated otherwise. In the writing exercises, the word limit is 150–200 words for the Extended curriculum and 100–150 words for the Core curriculum.

Copies of the IGCSE English as a Second Language syllabus 0510 is available from the University of Cambridge International Examinations (www.cie.org.uk).

Menu for the book

Theme	Unit	Exam focus	Unit focus
Leisure and entertainment	1	Reading exercise 1 *Skimming and scanning*	A Speaking and vocabulary, B Reading, C Language focus, D Speaking, E Further practice
	2	Reading exercise 2 *Detailed understanding*	A Speaking and vocabulary, B Reading, C Writing, D Speaking, E Reading, F Further practice
	3	Writing exercises 6 and 7 *Informal letter*	A Reading and speaking, B Writing and vocabulary, C Writing, D Speaking, E Further practice
	4	Listening *Short items*	A Listening and speaking, B Reading, C Language focus, D Speaking, E Listening, F Further practice
	5	Exam practice	Reading and writing exam exercises 1, 2, 6 and 7, and Listening exam part 1
Work and education	6	Reading exercise 2 *Detailed understanding*	A Reading, B Language focus, C Speaking, D Speaking, E Reading, F Further practice
	7	Reading and writing exercise 4 *Form-filling*	A Reading, B Writing, C Speaking, D Reading, E Writing, F Further practice
	8	Writing exercise 5, 6 and 7 *Formal writing*	A Spelling, B Reading, C Speaking, D Writing, E Speaking, F Further practice
	9	Listening *Exam part 3*	A Speaking, B Listening, C Writing, D Listening, E Speaking, F Reading, G Further practice
	10	Exam practice	Reading and writing exam exercises 2, 3, 6 and 7, and Listening exam Part 2
People and relationships	11	Reading exercises 1 and 2 *All skills*	A Speaking, B Reading, C Reading and vocabulary, D Speaking, E Writing, F Further practice
	12	Reading and writing exercises 4 and 5 *Note-taking and summary*	A Reading, B Writing, C Speaking and vocabulary, D Reading, E Writing, F Speaking, G Further practice
	13	Writing exercises 6 and 7 *All skills*	A Speaking, B Writing, C Reading, D Vocabulary, E Reading and writing, F Writing, G Speaking, H Further practice
	14	Listening *Exam part 2*	A Writing and speaking, B Listening, C Reading, D Speaking and vocabulary, E Listening, F Speaking, G Further practice
	15	Exam practice	Reading and writing exam exercises 1, 2, 4 and 5, and Listening exam
Ideas and the future	16	Reading exercises 1 and 2 *All skills*	A Speaking and vocabulary, B Reading, C Writing, D Vocabulary, E Reading, F Speaking, G Further practice
	17	Reading and writing exercises 3, 4 and 5 *Note-taking and summary*	A Speaking and vocabulary, B Reading, C Writing, D Speaking and vocabulary, E Reading, F Writing, G Speaking, H Further practice
	18	Writing exercises 6 and 7 *All skills*	A Speaking, B Writing, C Speaking and vocabulary, D Reading, E Writing, F Reading, G Speaking, H Writing, I Further practice
	19	Listening *Exam part 3*	A Speaking, B Listening, C Writing, D Listening, E Reading, F Speaking, G Further practice
	20	Exam practice	Sample paper

Acknowledgements

We are grateful to the following for permission to reproduce their photographs:

Associated Press p76; BEET Language Centre p41; Bettmann/Corbis p82 (Robert Wadlaw); Corbis: p11 (John Lund), p35 (Jennie Woodcock), p89 (Desmond Boylan), p93 (Jennie Woodcock), p97 (Mitchell Gerber), p105 (Ted Streshinsky), pp113, 119, 133 (Thom Lang); p140 (David Reed); p143 (Kevin Fleming); Arnald Desrochers p111; Digital Vision Ltd p18; Ecoscene/Rosemary Greenwood p128; Getty Images pp56, 62; Sally and Richard Greenhill p13; Robert Harding pp20, 31; Impact pp27, 84, 125, 129, 141; The Independent p37; Mary Evans Picture Library p105; Panos p151; popperfoto.com p85; Rex Features p113; Science Photo Library p74, Peter Shelley p38; S.I.N/Corbis p91; Christos Theodorides p53.

Cover image by courtesy of Jeremy Horner/CORBIS

We would like to thank the following for permission to use their material in either the original or adapted form:

ASDA magazine p49; Associated Press p76; AstraZeneca p112; BEET Language Centre pp42, 45, 46, 47; Alex Bellas p151; Britespot Publishing Solutions Ltd p89; Culinaria Italia published by Konemann p114; Cyprus Review p84, p96, p117; Cyprus Sunday Mail p53; Der Grune Punkt p77; English Heritage p19; Florence Nightingale Foundation p107; ©The Guardian pp17, 21; Guiness Media Inc. p82; HMSO (Licence C01W0000180), pp12, 13, 15; Independent Newspapers Ltd pp37, 38, 61, 113, 119; Karin Millson/Apex Publishing p26; Myriad Editions Ltd p146; NI Syndication London pp121, 125, 131, 135; Prospect Publishing Ltd pp31 – 32; Soma Akriton, Youth Organisation, Cyprus p103; TWINS Magazine p93; University of Cambridge Local Examinations Syndicate p39; VisitLondon.com p35; Voyager Magazine – PSP Communications p25; World Scout Bureau/Asia Pacific Region p98; World Association of Girl Guides and Girl Scouts p101.

Unit 1: *Focus on reading skills*

Exam Exercise 1

In this unit we will concentrate on skimming and scanning reading skills, which are particularly important in Exercise 1 of the IGCSE E2L Reading and Writing paper.

> In Exercise 1 of the IGCSE Reading and Writing paper, you need to be able to understand and respond to information presented in a variety of forms, such as notices, leaflets, signs, advertisements, timetables, and so on. There may be pictures or other visuals with the text and you need to give single word or short phrase answers.
>
> Marks = 8 Extended, 6 Core.

Ⓐ Speaking and vocabulary

1 What do the following words and phrases have in common? Add more words to the list.

free time   relaxation   entertainment

2 What do you enjoy doing in your free time? Make a list of things you enjoy and don't enjoy doing. Compare your lists with your partner's. Are they the same or different?

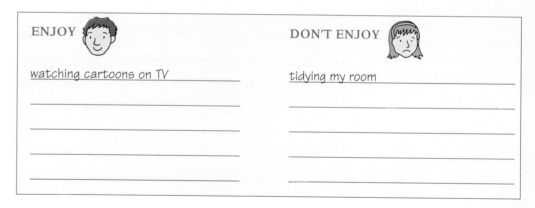

ENJOY

watching cartoons on TV
_____
_____
_____
_____

DON'T ENJOY

tidying my room
_____
_____
_____
_____

B Reading

3 When you want to find something quickly in a text, what do you do? Which reading skills do you use? When you read something for pleasure, such as a book or a magazine, do you read it in the same way? Are there any other 'ways' in which you can read a text?

4 Look at the advertisement for SONIKS products. Answer these two questions. You have 20 seconds!

a How many different products are advertised?

b Which product is the most expensive?

5 Which reading skill did you use to answer the questions in Exercise 4?

6 Answer the following question. Do *not* write anything yet.

  – Which product has the biggest percentage reduction?

7 Which of the following is the *best* answer to question 6? Is more than one answer possible? Why?

a The SONIKS baseball cap has the biggest percentage reduction.

b The product with the biggest percentage reduction is the SONIKS baseball cap.

c It's the SONIKS baseball cap.

d SONIKS baseball cap

e baseball cap

8 With your partner, ask and answer the following questions. You do *not* need to write anything yet.

a Which **three** products have normal shop prices of less than £10?

b How can you save an additional £10?

c Which product offers the biggest cash saving?

d How many SONIKS millennium games were sold in a month in the USA?

e Give **three** advantages of using www.SONIKS.com shopping

f Which product contains 100 cards?

g Which product is available in four different colours?

9 Write the answers to the questions in Exercise 8. Exchange your answers with a different partner. Check their answers. What should you be looking for?

NEW FROM —

SONIKS.com

COMPUTER GAMES

SONIKS millennium game at a discount price of £46.86!
(Normal shop price £49.98: Save 6%!)
This is the one that sold a million in a month in the USA! If you haven't got it already, now's your chance to get the most up-to-date visual effects to add-on to your SONIKS games.

SONIKS topic cards at a discount price of £25.12!
(Normal shop price £29.00: Save 13%!)
Share cards too easy now?! Move on to these fantastic SONIKS topic cards and beat the rest!

SONIKS tactics guide at a discount price of £3.85!
(Normal shop price £8.50: Save 55%!)
Hot tips and amazing ideas to extend the range of your SONIKS games.

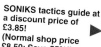

SONIKS share cards at a discount price of £22.35!
(Normal shop price £24.90: Save 10%!)
Loads of exciting fun and games with more than 100 share cards to use with your SONIKS games.

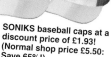

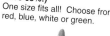

SONIKS baseball caps at a discount price of £1.93!
(Normal shop price £5.50: Save 65%!)
One size fits all! Choose from red, blue, white or green.

SONIKS cuddly toys at a discount price of £5.11!
(Normal shop price £5.99: Save 15%!)
Choose from the set of 6 SONIKS cuddly toys. Delightful presents for all ages.

SONIKS watches at a discount price of £9.99! (Normal shop price £19.99: Save 50%!)
Got all the games and add-on? Keep in front of the rest with a techno SONIKS digital watch with removable coloured straps and changeable dials. 5 colours and dials available.

FREE £10.00 OFFER!

You can save even more at our **www.SONIKS.com/shopping** website. Spend a minimum of £20.00 and get a voucher for £10.00 to use on your next visit. You also get a 21-day money-back, no questions asked guarantee, a secure server, and immediate e-mail confirmation of your order. Visit our website or phone 0800 123 9876 24 hours a day for help.

10 Have a quick look at the second text, SONIKS Picture CD, on page 5. Where might you find a text like this? Choose one or more answers from the list:

**a dictionary   an email   a newspaper   an encyclopaedia
a TV magazine   a children's magazine   a comic
a shop window   a leaflet**

11 What features does this SONIKS text have? What types of information does it contain? Copy and complete the table below:

TEXT FEATURES	TEXT INFORMATION
different sizes of script	prices

12 Put the following strategy points into a logical order. Be prepared to explain your order.

a Search likely sections of the text.

b Read the question.

c Underline the key word/s.

d Ask yourself what information the question is asking for.

13 Look at these questions based on the SONIKS Picture CD advertisement. Do *not* write anything yet. Find the key word or words in each question. Discuss your choices with your partner.

a What **three** things will you receive with your photographs?

b Name **four** things that you can do to your pictures with the SONIKART software.

c What do you need to do to order your CD?

d What alternative method is given for ordering the CD?

e How many rolls of film can you send with each order?

f How much extra should you pay for postage and packing?

g How long do you need to wait for your photos to arrive?

h What should you do if you do *not* wish to receive details of other products?

i What **two** methods of payment are available?

Get your photos on your home computer or laptop with SONIKS Picture CD!

SONIKS

PICTURE CD

SONIKS introduce a great new service for all you creative photography and computer fans out there! Now you can have all your most treasured photos on your PC for just **£1.00**. When you send your films to SONIKS for developing, for just £1.00 extra we will send you your SONIKS Picture CD – it's as simple as that! You'll also get a **FREE** interactive guide explaining how to view your pics, plus our incredible **SONIKART** software program, which allows you to edit your photos and create amazing special effects! You can crop them, enlarge them, stretch them, change the colours, add hair, remove spots, print them or e-mail them! The limit is your own imagination!

To order, simply complete and send us the order form below, along with your film (only one roll of film per order). You pay for your pics, £1.00 for the SONIKS Picture CD, and P&P (60p). Alternatively, take this advertisement with your film to your local SONIKS retailer.

HOW TO PAY
Make cheques payable to SONIKS Ltd, or complete your credit card details.

Please debit my VISA/MASTERCARD/AMEX card by
£ ....
Card number: ....
Expiry date: ....
Signature: ....
Mr/Ms: ....
Address: ....
....
................................Postcode: ....

Allow up to 14 days for delivery.
Data Protection Act: Sometimes we may wish to send you information about products which we feel may be of interest to you. Tick the box if you do NOT wish to receive such information ☐

14 Did you choose 'photographs' as the key word in question 13a, or 'pictures' in 13b? Why/Why not?

15 Was it possible to identify key words in every question? Sometimes you may not be able to decide, but usually there will be one or two words which will help you to identify where the answer is. Now answer the questions in Exercise 13. Keep your answers short, but remember to include all the information that the question asks for. Exchange your answers with your partner. Check your partner's answers.

 © Language focus: word-building

16 Notice the use of adjectives in the two SONIKS advertisements:

exciting fun and games

amazing ideas

removable coloured straps

free interactive guide

creative photography

Complete the sentence:

Adjectives are used to provide ...... about ......

17 Adjectives can often be formed from other parts of speech. Copy and complete the table below with the correct words. You may not be able to complete all the gaps.

ADJECTIVE	NOUN	ADVERB	VERB
exciting	excitement	excitingly	excite
amazing	amazment	amazingly	amaze
digital	digit	digitally	digitise
removable	removal		remove
delightful	delight	delightfully	delight
creative	creation	creatively	create
interactive	interaction	interactively	interact
incredible		incredibly	

18 What do you notice about the endings of the adjectives in Exercise 17? Look back at the two SONIKS advertisements and find more adjectives. Add them to your table and then complete the other parts of speech (noun, adverb, verb).

19 Using the table on page 6, make a list of the possible endings for adjectives. Then think of **three** more examples for each ending.

For example:

-ing   *interesting, fascinating, boring*

 D **Speaking: showing preference and making suggestions**

20 Look at this conversation between Maria and Christos.

Maria: Why don't we go into town and see if that new CD is out yet?

Christos: Yes, we could do that, but I'd rather go next week because I should be able to get some more money by then.

Maria: OK, let's go next week instead. But what are we going to do today ...?

The underlined phrases show preference or are making suggestions. Think of more examples of language which could be used. Copy and complete the table below and compare your ideas with your partner's.

MAKING SUGGESTIONS	SHOWING PREFERENCE
Why don't we ...?	I'd rather go ...

Usually when we show a preference for something we also give a reason:

I'd rather go next week because I should be able to get some more money by then.

Look at how **suggestion** and **preference** phrases are followed by infinitive, 'to' infinitive or gerund forms of the verb:

Why don't we + *do*?	Would you like + *to do*?	What/How about + *doing*?
Let's + *do*	I'd rather + *do*	What do you think about + *doing*?
I suggest we + *do*	I'd like + *to do*	I suggest + *doing*
Can't we + *do*?	I('d) prefer + *to do*	
I think we should + *do*		

! EXAM TIP

In the IGCSE interview, you may be asked to make suggestions and express preferences about a particular topic. Although it is important to speak accurately during the interview (and using set phrases like the ones practised in this unit will be very helpful), the most important thing is to talk effectively in a fluent manner. Avoid using slang, say 'yes', not 'yeah', and try to use full sentences whenever possible.

21 Work with your partner. For each of the following examples, one of you makes a suggestion, and the other gives a preference and a reason. Try to use a variety of the phrases from the Language box on page 7.

Example: buying a new pair of trainers or putting your money in the bank

Maria: Why don't you buy that pair of trainers we saw in town?

Christos: No, I don't think so, Maria. I'd prefer to save my money for the summer holidays.

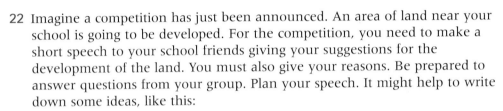

a going on holiday to Australia or Iceland

b eating Italian or Chinese food for dinner

c listening to classical or hip hop music

d going to the cinema or the disco

e playing football or going swimming

22 Imagine a competition has just been announced. An area of land near your school is going to be developed. For the competition, you need to make a short speech to your school friends giving your suggestions for the development of the land. You must also give your reasons. Be prepared to answer questions from your group. Plan your speech. It might help to write down some ideas, like this:

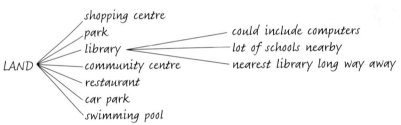

 E Further practice

23 Find some examples of advertisements similar to the ones you have read in this unit. Study them carefully and then write 6–8 questions for your partner to answer. Remember that in Exercise 1 of the IGCSE Reading and Writing paper the questions require you to find short factual details.

24 Underline some sentences from your advertisements which contain adjectives. Then make a table like the one in Exercise 17 and write the noun, adverb and verb for each adjective (where possible).

25 You are going to the cinema with two friends. There is a choice of films: a comedy, a love story, and a sci-fi film. With two partners, suggest which film to go and see, and give a reason. Then make arrangements to meet.

26 Look at the African safari advertisement on page 9. Find the key word/s in the questions. Then write your answers.

a What is the minimum price for the African Safari? £1,355

b Name an activity included in the African Safari? camping with the stars

c How long is the African Safari? 6 nights

d How far is the Victoria Falls Hotel from the airport? 30 km

e What can you see from the hotel? breathtaking water, surrounded by jacaranda trees

f Where will you sleep on day 2? campsite

g Which hotels offer swimming facilities? Zimbabwe National Hotel, Plaza Hotel

h Which hotel is said to be among the best in Africa? Victoria Falls hotel

i When will you get the chance to see animals living in their natural environment? Day 5

j On which day are you offered the chance to go shopping? Day 6

k What meals are included in the basic price? B and B meal basis

l Which airline will fly you to Africa? Air Zimbabwe

AFRICAN SAFARI

A night in the African rainforest, camping under the stars, right next to the mighty Victoria Falls in Zimbabwe, is just one of the many never-to-be-forgotten experiences of our latest offer to Weekly News readers. 6 nights of pure African luxury in Zimbabwe's best hotels, with 5 star class and total comfort.

Day 1: The 5★ Victoria Falls Hotel will cater for all your needs during your first day in Africa after the 30 km drive from the new international airport. Located only minutes from the falls, the hotel has splendid views of the breathtaking waters, and is surrounded by jacaranda trees and beautifully cared for gardens. This hotel is regarded as one of the best on the African continent, and has been voted the best in Zimbabwe by our panel of regular visitors.

Day 2: Your night under the stars, within a few minutes' walk of the cascading waters of the Victoria Falls. Our purpose-built campsite retains the comfort and luxury of the main hotel, whilst offering our guests a chance to savour the atmosphere of the rainforest. Your evening starts with a sumptuous barbecue cooked by our head chef, followed by a programme of African music and dance. Then, as the moon rises and the stars shine, you retire to your tent to sleep or to listen to the fascinating sounds of the African rainforest. An experience never to be forgotten!

Days 3–4: The 5★ Zimbabwe National Hotel will accommodate you in the heart of the Zimbabwean wilderness. By jeep from your camp site near the falls, you arrive midday via the Zambezi river. The hotel complex offers you every amenity you would expect from a **5*** luxury hotel, including golf, tennis, squash, badminton, swimming in one of three open-air pools, bowls, or full use of our health suite. In the evening, enjoy our international menu, visit the casino, or relax in the gardens.

Days 5–6: Arrive by helicopter at the 5* Plaza Hotel, only 20 minutes' drive from the airport. The Plaza is located near to the Zimbabwean National Game Reserve, and day 5 includes an amazing safari to see some of the world's most exotic animals in their natural habitats. Your final day can be spent in the luxurious surroundings of the hotel, or you can make a shopping trip into town. The hotel itself offers a full range of **5★** facilities, including its own cinema, as well as a pool complex with diving boards.

Included in this special offer: 6 nights in 5 hotel accommodation. Depart from London Stansted Airport. B&B meal basis (for HB, add £250). Price is per person based on two people sharing (add £450 for single room). Scheduled flights with Air Zimbabwe.*

from **only**
£1,355
per person

27 Read the 'New Rating System' notice and answer the questions which follow.

New Rating System

Global rating system for computer and video games

There are two parts to the new system: an age rating and an indication of the content of the game. In future, all games, whether for computer or video, must feature an age rating on the front cover indicating that the game is only suitable for users aged at or above the particular age listed.

The new age brackets are:

3+	7+	12+	16+	18+

Additionally, the game box should feature one or more descriptors, including the type of content. This descriptor will normally appear on the reverse of the box, and the content will always be appropriate to the age rating.

The new content descriptors include:

 Violence

Game contains descriptions of violence

 Fear

Game may be frightening for young children

 Bad language

Game contains bad language

Discrimination

Game contains depictions of, or material which may encourage, discrimination

The new system has been based on existing systems throughout the world, and consultations with parents, consumers and religious groups. It has been designed to meet the various cultural standards and attitudes of the participating countries. While there are minor local variations in some countries, it is hoped that the new system will eventually supersede existing national systems.

Source: *The Game*, July-August 2003

a In which countries will the new rating system apply? *All the countries*

b Where on the box can the content descriptors be found? *on the reverse of the box*

c What does a spider symbol indicate? *game may be frightening for young children*

d How was the new system developed? *indicating that the game is only suitable for users aged*

e Why was the number of countries involved in the system a possible problem? *designed To meet various cultural standards*

f Which word in the final paragraph has a similar meaning to 'replace'? *supersede*

Leisure and entertainment

Unit 2: *Focus on reading skills*

Exam Exercise 2
In this unit we will again concentrate on skimming and scanning reading skills, as well as on identifying the key words in questions.

> In Exercise 2 of the IGCSE Reading and Writing paper, you may be required to show more detailed understanding of a longer and more demanding text than in Exercise 1, such as a report or a newspaper or magazine article. Usually there will be a picture or other visuals with the text. Sometimes you will need to infer information from the text.
>
> Marks = 14 Extended, 10 Core.

A Speaking and vocabulary

1   Find the names of ten different types of television programme in the wordbox. The words are either horizontal or vertical – not diagonal. Check your answers with your partner.

Q	G	H	N	B	M	U	S	I	C	O	U	A	O
W	F	J	K	H	X	Z	P	Y	O	R	E	D	B
E	D	K	C	A	R	T	O	O	N	X	Z	K	W
R	C	L	O	U	N	S	R	A	D	B	N	I	E
D	O	C	U	M	E	N	T	A	R	Y	M	E	S
T	M	M	M	Y	W	E	R	V	A	J	U	N	T
Y	E	N	L	G	S	F	L	L	M	M	E	O	E
U	D	B	P	V	D	W	W	E	A	T	H	E	R
I	Y	H	O	R	R	O	R	P	J	P	T	Z	N
O	S	V	Z	C	R	A	S	H	F	D	B	N	D
P	A	C	X	F	T	Q	J	A	Z	F	A	I	X

2   Do you have all the different types of programme you found in the wordbox in your country? Are there any types of programme you have which are not in the wordbox? Are there any types of programme in the wordbox which you do not have, and which you would like to have in your own country? Which of the programmes do you like watching? Which ones don't you like? Why?

3 How much TV do you normally watch each day? What does it depend on? Look back at the list you made in Exercise 2 in Unit 1. How much time do you spend doing the activities on your list? Copy and complete the table below and then compare and discuss with your partner what you have written.

ACTIVITIES	MINUTES PER WEEK
watching cartoons on TV	
tidying my room	

4 Look at this graph, which shows the number of minutes per week spent on various activities by young people in Britain.

▶ **2.1** Time spent by young people on activities.

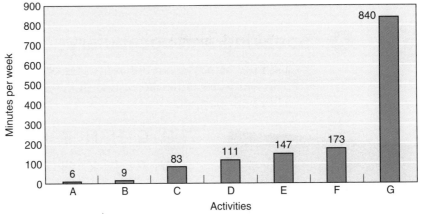

Source: Adapted from *Young People in Britain*, Foreign and Commonwealth Office, London, 1999

Which activities (A–G) do you think are represented in the graph? Choose from the list below. Be careful! There are two extra activities which you do not need to use. Discuss with your partner and then write down which activities A–G represent.

gardening   playing a musical instrument   writing and drawing playing sport   youth clubs, girl guides and scouts   charity work watching TV   reading books and magazines playing computer games

Compare your choices with the ones your teacher gives you. Does anything surprise you? Which activities didn't you choose? Why not?

B Reading

5 Think back to Unit 1. Which reading skills are the most useful in answering questions in Exercise 1 of the IGCSE Reading and Writing paper? Complete the sentences:

a Skim reading is when you read something to …

b Scan reading is when you read something to …

6 You are going to read a passage from a magazine published by the British government. It gives information about various aspects of the lives of young people in Britain today. Before you read the passage, what differences do you think there might be between the activities of young people aged 11–15 years and those aged 15–24? Be prepared to say why.

7 Before you read, look at these words and phrases which have been removed from the passage. Match each word or phrase with one of the definitions given. Discuss your choices with your partner. Use your dictionary for help.

WORD		DEFINITION	
a	a great deal of	i	money which is not needed for essentials (food, rent, bills, etc.)
b	a host of	ii	prove
c	confirm	iii	be likely to do something
d	disposable income	iv	large amounts of
e	insufficient	v	activities
f	pursuits	vi	a large quantity of
g	range	vii	not enough
h	tend to	viii	variety

Young people in Britain

Home is the central focus of most young people's lives, particularly those who are still attending school. In the younger age group, from 10 to 16, children are at the age when they are strongly influenced by their friends, sometimes influenced by their parents, partially influenced by teachers, and altogether affected by (1) youth culture influences outside the home. When they are not at school, eating, or doing their homework, young people in their teens (2) spend a lot of their time in their own neighbourhoods with friends, either in the streets or parks or in each other's homes. They tend not to spend their time organising or participating in clearly defined leisure (3).

Surveys show that only relatively few young people regularly attend youth clubs, although there are sufficient attendances to result in an enormous (4) of organisations established across Britain. The younger age group of 11–15-year-olds most often attend youth clubs and centres, although less than 20 per cent of this population are regular attenders. Most young people are more interested in general social interactions that they can pick up and drop with ease – particularly activities that do not cost money. Lack of their own money in the younger age groups means that (5) time is spent with friends, window-shopping in town, cycling or skateboarding.

In the older age group, those who are still at school, or who are unemployed and on relatively low-paid training schemes, have (6) income to do what they please and are therefore restricted in their activities. Over 60 per cent of young people aged 15–24 have a (7) of less than £50 per week. Young men and women who have started earning properly tend to join in pursuits that (8) their status as adults, such as spending time in pubs, going to dances, concerts, discos and the cinema.

Source: Adapted from *Young People in Britain*, Foreign and Commonwealth Office, London, 1999

8 Read the passage and decide which word or phrase in the pairs below best completes each gap. Check your answers with your partner.

1 insufficient/a host of

2 tend to/confirm

3 range/pursuits

4 disposable income/range

5 a host of/a great deal of

6 insufficient/pursuits

7 a great deal of/disposable income

8 confirm/tend to

! EXAM TIP

Notice that words from the passage are often rephrased in the questions, for example 'central focus' is 'centre of interest' in question 9a.

9 Read the following questions and find the key word/s in each one. You do *not* need to write anything yet.

a What is the centre of interest in most young people's lives? *homes*

b Who are children in the younger age group most influenced by? *friends*

c What other things influence children aged 10–16? *friends , parents , teachers*

d When teenagers are not studying or eating, what are they most likely to be doing? *spending time with friends*

e What are 10–16-year-olds *not* likely to be doing in their free time? *attend to youth club*

f Why is there an enormous range of youth organisations in Britain? *less young people attend youth clubs*

g How often do the majority of young people attend youth clubs? *they do not regularly attend*

h What is the result of 11–15-year-olds not having much money? *cycling , window shopping , skateboarding*

i Why are people in the older age group limited in their pursuits? *they need to earn money need income is insufficient*

j What percentage of people aged 15–24 have a disposable income of more than £50 per week? *40% or below*

k Name **four** activities which older employed people participate in. *pubs , concert , discos , cinema*

10 Look back at the passage. Find the words you noted.

11 In some parts of the exam, you need to write more than just a few words in your answer. Which of the following is the *best* answer for question 9i? Why?

a Because of their income.

b Because their income is insufficient.

c People in the older age group are limited in their pursuits because they have insufficient income.

d Because they don't have enough income so can't do what they want.

12 Now write complete answers to the questions in Exercise 9. Exchange answers with your partner. Check your partner's answers. What should you be looking for?

C Writing: adverb phrases

Look at these **adverb phrases** taken from the passage you have read:

a <u>strongly</u> influenced by their friends
b <u>partially</u> influenced by teachers
c <u>clearly</u> defined leisure pursuits
d <u>regularly</u> attend youth clubs
e <u>particularly</u> activities that do not cost money
f <u>relatively</u> low-paid training schemes
g have started earning <u>properly</u>

The underlined words are all **adverbs**. Adverbs can modify verbs and adjectives, as well as other adverbs, and can show a degree of something.

13 Complete each sentence with a suitable phrase containing an adverb.

Examples: *Mario's brother was injured in the accident, <u>but he was not too badly hurt.</u>*
The film was much too long <u>and was incredibly boring!</u>

a Elena thought the new café would be cheap but …

b Look at that house which caught fire last week. It's been …

c Siphiwe usually plays well but today he's …

d When Rasheed and Ranya arrived at their hotel, they were surprised to see that everything …

e The mountains in the interior of the island were …

f The room had been painted in a strange way: the walls were …

g George did not tell anyone that he was going to visit us. He arrived …

h Only Sayeed agreed with Fiona. Everyone else …

i The results of the survey show that older people …

j Tutaleni tried to be independent but his elder sister Nangula …

D # Speaking: would do/wouldn't do

14 Look at the following information about young people in Britain. Talk to your partner about the amount of pocket money people of different ages receive in Britain. How do the figures compare with your country? How much pocket money do you receive? Is it enough?

▶ **2.2** Average weekly pocket money (£). Source: Adapted from *Young People in Britain*, Foreign and Commonwealth Office, London, 1999

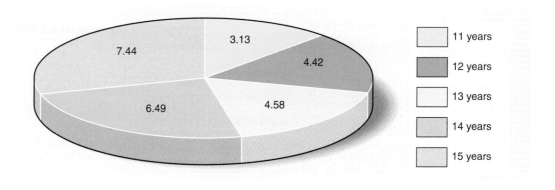

15 How would you ask your parents for more pocket money? Would you need to give them a reason? Discuss with your partner and make a list of possible phrases.

Examples: *Is there any chance I could have …?*
Do you think it would be possible to have …?

16 Suppose you urgently needed some extra money. Would you be prepared to 'earn' extra money instead of asking your parents for it? How? What would you not be prepared to do to earn money? Discuss with your partner. Try to use some of the phrases below. Add some more phrases to the lists.

WOULDN'T DO	WOULD DO
I certainly wouldn't ever do ...	I wouldn't mind doing ...
... is the last thing I'd do to earn money!	I'd be quite happy to do ...
Doing ... is something I'd never do.	I wouldn't have a problem in doing ...
I can't imagine myself ever doing ...	Doing ... is fine by me.
There's no way I'd ever do ...	I would enjoy doing ...

 E Reading

You are going to read a newspaper article about beaches in Italy. Before you read, answer the following questions with your partner.

17 Have you ever been to a beach for a holiday? What kind of things do you like doing on the beach? What things do you think you should be able to buy on the beach? Why? Are there any beaches in your country? If so, what things are sold on the beaches? Do you buy them? What are the advantages and disadvantages of living near a beach?

18 The following words appear in the text. Discuss what they mean with your partner. Use your dictionary for help.

  a rationed   *limited*

  b shrivelled

  c vacationers   *hoildayers*

  d simultaneously   *two or more things happen the same time together*

  e congestion   *jams*

  f abandoned   *left behind*

  g flippers

  h phenomenon

19 Scan the text and find the words from Exercise 18. Do the meanings you discussed with your partner make sense?

Seaside scrum, Italian style

Italians can joyfully unfold their towels on one of the longest and most beautiful coastlines in the world. The only problem is that they are being rationed to just 50cm of space each. The room for lying on some beaches has shrivelled as 20 million vacationers simultaneously try to get away from it all. Large areas of Mediterranean and Adriatic sand have vanished beneath forests of bodies which must stay still or risk banging into their neighbour.

Congestion has forced football and volleyball activities to be abandoned in favour of handheld electronic games. Swimmers can no longer use their flippers. Peace and quiet do not exist. From Liguria and Tuscany in the west, Sicily in the south and Rimini in the east, the average space is under 50cm and narrowing fast, according to Legambiente, Italy's environmental group.

Those people who choose to travel from the cities to the coast are being forced to sit in their vehicles in traffic jams which are longer than 130 kilometres. This is a phenomenon which Italians accept as normal.

However, the recent crush appears worse than ever. Some towns have appointed beach police to maintain order, with mixed success. On some beaches, the prices charged for the usual beach products such as umbrellas, ice creams and drinks have rocketed. Furthermore, the number of people walking up and down the beaches selling these items, plus a whole list of other 'beach-essential' products, has increased enormously. In Alassio, on the Ligurian coast, it has been calculated that beach sellers approach the average visitor 107 times a day, or every four minutes during peak time.

Source: Adapted from an article by Rory Carroll, *The Guardian*, 11 August 2000

20 Answer the following questions. Remember to identify the key word/s in each question first.

   a How many people visit the beaches at any one time? *20 million*

   b What happens if people on the beach move too much? *They may bang into their neighbours*

   c Why is it impossible to do any sports activities on the beach? *the average space is under 50 cm so you get congestion*

   d How do people entertain themselves now on the beach? *electronic games*

   e What is the job of the beach police? *to maintain order, with mixed success*

   f What other problems, apart from lack of space, are evident on Italian beaches? *changes are high*

   g Copy and complete the Italian beaches fact form.

Italian beaches – Fact form

Space per person on beach: *50 cm*

Number of people on holiday: *20 million*

Coastal problem areas: *Liguria, Tuscany, Rimini, Sicily*

Length of jams: *130 km*

Visits by beach sellers per day: *107*

F **Further practice**

21 Copy and complete the table below. You may not be able to fill all the gaps.

NOUN	ADJECTIVE	ADVERB
strength	strong	strongly
part	partial	partially
clarity	clear	clearly
regularity	regular	regularly
/	particular	particularly
relation	relative	relatively
/	incredible	incredibly
total	total	totally
completeness	complete	completely

All the words appear in some form in the text you have read.

22 Write a holiday postcard to someone in your family in which you:

- describe the place where you are staying
- ask for more spending money

Write in complete sentences and limit your writing to about 75 words.

23 Draw a graph similar to the one in Exercise 4 for your own weekly activities. Then write a short paragraph about the information in your graph. Write about 60 words.

24 Read the leaflet about Stonehenge and answer the questions which follow.

Prehistoric Wonder of the World

Discover one of the world's greatest prehistoric monuments!

As old as the great temples and pyramids of Egypt, Stonehenge exerts a mysterious fascination.

Our complimentary audio tour in nine languages (subject to availability) will tell you all you need to know about the most intriguing and remarkable monument in the British Isles.

Make time to explore the extensive prehistoric landscape around Stonehenge. Some of these mysterious remains of ceremonial and domestic structures are older than the monument itself. Situated nearby is Old Sarum, where you can discover the remains of an Iron Age Hillfort, royal castle and cathedral. You can also visit the well-stocked gift shop or sample the delicious refreshments at the Stonehenge Kitchen.

Source: English Heritage

a   Find at least **ten** adjectives in the text.

b   Copy the table below and fill in your adjectives. Then try to complete the 'Antonyms' and 'Synonyms' columns. You may not be able to complete all the gaps in the table. Use your dictionary for help.

ADJECTIVES	ANTONYMS	SYNONYMS
greatest	worst	best

c   Choose some of the adjectives and use them in sentences of your own.

Unit 3: *Focus on writing skills*

Exam Exercises 6 and 7

In this unit we will concentrate on writing an informal letter, which may be required in Exercise 6 or Exercise 7 of the IGCSE Reading and Writing paper.

> *In Exercises 6 and 7 of the IGCSE Reading and Writing paper, you need to show that you can communicate clearly, accurately and appropriately, and use a variety of grammatical structures and vocabulary. Paragraphing, punctuation and spelling are also important, as is writing in the correct style (informal or formal).*
>
> Marks = 18 Extended, 10 Core.

A Reading and speaking

1 What is fast food? Try to put the following words into two groups: fast food and traditional food. There are no right or wrong answers.

**burger   hot dog   goulash   sandwich   vegetable pie
rice   moussaka   onion soup   falafel   samosa**

How did you decide on what to put in each group?

2 Do you like fast food? Why/Why not? What is your favourite food?

3 You are going to read a newspaper article called 'Pasta gives way to present'. What do you think the article might be about? Study the headline carefully: what do you notice about the words 'pasta' and 'present'?

4 Before you read the article, discuss with your partner whether the following statements are true or false:

a McDonald's has 25% of the Italian fast food market.

b There are 243 McDonald's restaurants in Italy.

c McDonald's sells pizza in Italy.

d A Big Mac contains more than 600 calories.

5   Scan the text and check your answers to Exercise 4.

Pasta gives way to present

McDonald's and Burger King have breached Italy's final frontier: pasta, pizza and mamma's cooking are succumbing to foreign fast food. Decades of resistance by family-owned bars, pizzerias and restaurants look like ending in defeat with the announcement that the two chains are doubling their outlets in Italy. A huge investment is under way, based on evidence that Italians are ready to abandon eating habits once considered immutable.

The US-owned McDonald's and British-owned Burger King – for years stalled at 5% of the market – are determined to bring Italy up to the European average of 25%. Within two years McDonald's intends to open 200 restaurants, most of them in central and southern Italy, which were considered the heartlands of the Mediterranean diet. Burger King, which did not have a single franchise until last year, plans to open more than 100. They expect to expand at the expense not of each other but of traditional restaurants.

McDonald's says the turnover at its existing 243 restaurants jumped by almost 20% last year. That is just scratching the surface, says Felice Invernizzi, marketing director of McDonald's Italia. Two months ago the chain launched its first pizza in Italy, called Pizza Mia. Sold by the slice, it has been a hit, despite purists' anguish. Burger King is bullish after cutting a deal with the pizza chain Spizzico, which can tap into a network of restaurants owned by its parent company, Autogrill.

'It is the globalisation of the palate,' La Repubblica mourned. The newspaper printed graphics showing how long it took to serve a Big Mac (90 seconds) and eat it (10 minutes). Breakdowns of ingredients and a calorie count (610) were accompanied by warnings from leading gourmets.

Edoardo Raspelli was sent on a field trip to McDonald's and Burger King in Milan. Having seen the future, he declared that it did not work. 'It takes a big effort to imagine this food as healthy. The ambience was mechanical, the chips like cardboard and the bread poor. I found it alienating and vulgar.'

Source: Adapted from an article by Rory Carroll. *The Guardian Weekly*, 11 May 2000

6   Now read the text more carefully and find the answers to the following questions. You do *not* need to write anything yet.

   a   By how much do McDonald's and Burger King hope to increase their market share?

   b   Where does McDonald's plan to open its restaurants?

   c   Why is this surprising?

   d   What will suffer as a result of the expansion of McDonald's and Burger King?

   e   How successful has Pizza Mia been?

   f   What is Spizzico?

   g   How long does it take to serve and eat a Big Mac?

   h   How does Raspelli describe the food in fast food restaurants?

7   Compare your ideas with your partner's. When you have agreed, write complete answers for each question.

B Writing and vocabulary

8 *Student A:* Find these words and phrases in the article. What do you think they mean? Use the context and your dictionary for help.

a breached (paragraph 1) *broken into*

b succumbing to (1) *spread out*

c decades (1) *ten years*

d outlets (1) *shop sell old products which are cheap*

e immutable (1) *impossible, wouldn't happen*

f stalled (2) *stop*

g turnover (3)

h palate (4) *taste*

Student B: Find these words and phrases in the article. What do you think they mean? Use the context and your dictionary for help.

a launched (paragraph 3) *started*

b purists' anguish (3)

c bullish (3) *straight, firm decision*

d cutting a deal (3) *making agreement*

e tap into (3)

f gourmets (4) *very decorated, smell, expensive*

g field trip (5)

h ambience (5) *atmosphere*

9 With your partner, discuss the meaning of the words and phrases in Exercise 8. Make sure you understand your partner's words and phrases as well as your own.

10 With your partner, choose ten words or phrases from the 16 you have discussed. Use each of your choices in a complete sentence in order to show its meaning.

C Writing: informal letter

11 What is your opinion about fast food restaurants taking over from traditional restaurants? What are the advantages and disadvantages of each type of restaurant? It might help if you concentrate on two restaurants that you know. Copy and complete the table listing the advantages and disadvantages of fast food and traditional restaurants.

FAST FOOD RESTAURANT		TRADITIONAL RESTAURANT	
Advantages	Disadvantages	Advantages	Disadvantages
quick service	not v. healthy	*Taste nicer*	*take quite a long time*

12 Look at this **exam-type question**. What exactly do you have to do? What should you not include in your answer? Discuss with your partner. Do *not* write anything yet.

> You have recently been to a new fast food restaurant in your town. Write a letter to a friend, telling him or her about your visit. In your letter you should:
> - explain where the restaurant is, when you went there, and why
> - describe the restaurant and its atmosphere
> - say what you ate and what you thought of the food
>
> Your letter should be about 150–200 words long (Extended) or 100–150 words long (Core).

13 What would be the best way to begin and end a letter like this? With your partner, make a list of possible opening and closing phrases for an informal letter.

OPENING PHRASES	CLOSING PHRASES
Hi Mark!	Best wishes
How are you?	Your sincerely

14 Look at this letter written by a student in response to the question in Exercise 12. There are some problems with it. What are they? With your partner, identify (a) the language errors, and (b) the problems with the information contained in the letter. Do *not* rewrite the letter.

Hello friend

I got your letter some days ago. How are you? I hope your well. I am very well and I am enjoy my holydays which have started before 2 days. My family are good and I am busy getting ready for to go away on the weekend on the mountins. I have taken good marks in my school tests but my mum and dad as usually they tell to me that I must to work more hard next year because it is my finaly year at school. I really enjoy the school but I think next year is going to be very hard for me because I will have to work very hard all the year. Guess what? A new burger restaurant was openning in my town and I went there with Marco and Jasper the last night. We stayed there until very late at night and we had to walk home because there was no buses! We had good food and the music too was wonderful. We will go there next time you will visit me and I hope to do so very soon. Write me back when you have free time won't you.

Yours faithfully

Felipe

15 Write your own answer to the exam-type question in Exercise 12. Take care to answer the question properly and do not include any irrelevant information. Check your work carefully for language errors, and count how many words you have written. Exchange your writing with your partner. Check your partner's letter. What should you be looking for?

D Speaking: expressing opinions

16 Look at this short conversation. The underlined phrases express opinions.

Anna: <u>I strongly believe that</u> fast food restaurants are here to stay.

Terry: <u>I honestly don't agree with that.</u> I am sure that people are beginning to realise how unhealthy fast food is.

Anna: But it's so convenient! <u>I can't imagine</u> people giving that up.

Terry: <u>I'm not so sure about that.</u>

With your partner, make a list of other phrases which you could use to express your opinion.

> **OPINION PHRASES**
>
> I strongly believe that ...
>
> I honestly don't agree with that.
>
> I can't imagine ...
>
> I'm not so sure about that.

17 Earlier in this unit you made a list of the advantages and disadvantages of fast food and traditional restaurants. Now imagine that you have to discuss these advantages and disadvantages with your teacher. What is your opinion? Use some of the phrases from Exercise 16, and your ideas from Exercise 11, to prepare for your discussion.

E Further practice

18 Read the text 'Water works' and answer the following questions.

a   What is the recommended amount of water to be drunk daily?   8

b   According to the text, is there anything wrong with tap water?   none

c   Give **two** suggested health benefits of drinking mineral water.   break up kidney stones

d   How many different standards must French mineral water meet?   8

e   Which French mineral water is recommended for use with baby food?   Evian

f   Why should mineral water be drunk before it is more than a few days old?

> **! EXAM TIP**
>
> In the IGCSE examination exercises 6 and 7, up to 9 marks are awarded for content, and up to 9 marks for language (5 + 5 in the Core papers). *Content* refers to the relevance and development of ideas; *language* refers to style and accuracy.

Water works

We are still not drinking enough water to maintain good health, according to a recent survey. Nearly three-fifths of the population only drink between one and four glasses of water daily – half the recommended amount.

But what's wrong with tap water? Nothing, in a word. But special health claims are made for mineral water. Some highly mineralised brands – such as Contrex in France, Fiuggi in Italy, and Radenska in Slovenia – are said to break up kidney stones. Others, renowned for their bicarbonate level – such as Fachingen in Germany, Ferrarelle in Italy, and Vichy Catalan in Spain – are said to aid digestion.

Your average British doc may find this a bit hard to swallow, but the French take a different view. Mineral water deemed to be *d'intérêt public* has to meet eight criteria agreed by the Ministry of Health, the Academy of Medicine and the Ministry of Mines.

The Good Water Guide (Rosendale Press) highlights the health promoting properties of these famous French names:

Contrex: sold with heavy emphasis on its diuretic properties, 'the slimmer's mineral water', originates from Contrexville. Fashionable Parisians have long visited the famous spa town to swig a litre or two.

Evian: ideal for diluting other drinks, its low mineral content makes it a suitable family table water ideal for mixing baby formula.

Saint-Yorre: from the Vichy basin, this is renowned as a digestive aid and a powerful thirst quencher.

Vittel: Grande Source Vittel waters 'boast a combination of calcium, magnesium and sulphates' and are 'beneficial to the kidneys, liver and gall bladder'.

Now for the health warning: always drink mineral water within a day or two to prevent bacterial contamination. *The Good Water Guide* explains that, rather like yoghurt, mineral water is 'live', i.e. it contains bacteria. It adds: 'This is no cause for alarm. That is where the real benefit comes from.'

Source: Adapted from *Voyager*, July/August 2000

19 Write your answer to this **exam-type question**:

You have recently cooked a meal for some members of your family. Write a letter to a friend, telling him or her about the meal. In your letter you should:

- explain why you cooked the meal
- say where you ate the meal, and with whom
- describe what you ate, and what everyone thought of the food

Your letter should be about 150–200 words long for the Extended curriculum, 100-150 words long for the Core.

20 Write a description of your favourite restaurant, or imagine one. Refer to its location, the layout of the furniture, the music and décor, the types of food, and give it a name. Write about 150–200 words for the Extended curriculum and 100–150 words for the Core curriculum.

Shellfish in Oman

The diverse riches of the sea have always played a significant role in Oman's economy and the lifestyle of her people. The nation's fishing industry continues to increase in importance as research into its marine life grows stronger.

An animal that is of enormous importance to the south-eastern coast of Oman is the *abalone*, a shellfish that has become the centre of a multi-million dollar industry.

Once, abalone shellfish were brought to the surface in the hope that the soft tissue contained beautiful pearls. Today, the shellfish are caught for a different reason – restaurant menus! The fresh white shellfish has a distinctive and much admired flavour and is the most highly valued product from Omani waters. It is fished exclusively along the shores of Dhofar.

This distinctive shellfish has only one shell, unlike other shellfish which have two. The shell is extremely beautiful. Light is diffracted by geometrically arranged crystals within the shell, creating a wonderful shine. The shells of several abalone can be used for decorative purposes, and to make jewellery and buttons.

Abalone live in shallow marine waters with rocky bottom conditions. Young abalone shelter in small groups, holding on to the undersides of medium-sized boulders, whereas the adults live grouped up to a dozen together in rocky cracks. They can only survive successfully in areas where cold, nutritious water rises from the sea bed. There, in the shallow, brightly lit conditions, the abalone shellfish live.

The environmental requirements for cool water conditions are rarely met, and, as a result, the geographical occurrence and extent of abalone fisheries worldwide is extremely restricted.

The coast of Dhofar in Oman is one of the special environments that support abalone populations. The southern shore of Oman experiences monsoon winds across the surface of the sea from April to September. As these winds skim the surface, the rich cold water from the depths of the Arabian Sea can easily rise and move towards the shore.

Abalone are harvested after the monsoon period, between October and March. Fishermen dive to a depth of ten metres assisted only by a face mask and, perhaps, fins. Groups of up to ten men search the sea bed for abalone-encrusted boulders and deftly remove the shells using a knife, before coming up for air. A good diver searches for large adults and will collect up to 600 specimens per day. In order to do this, the diver may have to cover an area in excess of 100 square metres.

Source: Adapted from 'New angles on abalone 'by Karin Millson, *Tribute*, 1990

21 Read the article 'Shellfish in Oman' and answer the questions which follow.

a Why is Oman's fishing industry continuing to expand?

b Why was the abalone shellfish originally important?

c Where is the only place that the abalone is obtained from?

d In what way is the abalone different from other shellfish?

e How do the habitats of young and adult abalone differ?

f What type of water do abalone need to live in?

g What two pieces of equipment do the abalone divers always use?

h What extra piece of equipment do some divers use?

Unit 4: *Focus on listening skills*

Exam Part 1

In this unit we will concentrate on the skills you need for Part 1 of the IGCSE Listening paper.

> *You need to show that you can understand and respond to information presented in a variety of forms, and select information which is relevant.*

Track 1

A Listening and speaking

1 How many different methods of transport can you and your partner think of? Make a list.

METHODS OF TRANSPORT

2   There are ten different methods of transport hidden in the wordbox. How many can you find? Are they the same as the ones you thought of in Exercise 1? The words in the box are written horizontally, vertically and diagonally.

B	M	N	E	V	C	A	E
U	I	E	H	G	A	W	K
S	O	C	O	A	B	C	I
R	T	P	Y	H	A	A	B
C	D	Z	C	C	L	M	R
S	F	A	G	J	L	P	O
V	O	S	T	A	O	E	T
C	F	E	R	R	O	R	O
I	Q	D	A	K	N	L	M
Y	T	C	I	R	N	C	G
P	L	A	N	E	V	X	S

3   Which method of transport do you think is the best for going on holiday? Why? Does it depend on the type of holiday? Discuss with your partner.

4   Make a list of the advantages and disadvantages for some of the methods of transport in Exercise 2.

METHOD	ADVANTAGES	DISADVANTAGES
car	stop when and where you like	traffic jams

5   In Exercises 3 and 4, did you consider the cost of each method? With your partner, rank the methods 1–10, with 1 being the most expensive and 10 the cheapest. What factors do you need to think about when deciding on the cost of each method?

6   You are going to listen to four people talking about their experiences of different methods of transport. The first time you listen, answer these questions:

   a   Which methods of transport are being talked about?

   b   Which of the people enjoyed themselves?

   c   Which speaker does *not* mention the name of a country or town?

7   The methods of transport are not actually mentioned by the speakers. What clues helped you to identify each one? Context? Vocabulary (key word/s)?

8   Listen carefully again to each speaker. As you listen, answer the following questions:

   Speaker 1

   a   Where exactly did the speaker wait for the train?

   b   How many people were with the speaker?

   c   How did the family feel before 8.30?

   d   What made the speaker and his family become anxious?

   e   What did the speaker do at 9.00?

   f   What mistake had the speaker made?

Speaker 2

    a   Why was the speaker going up in a balloon?

    b   How old is the speaker now?

    c   Why did the speaker feel uncomfortable about the balloon trip?

    d   How long was the balloon trip?

    e   How did the speaker feel once the balloon had taken off?

Speaker 3

    a   What two advantages convinced the speaker to travel by coach?

    b   How many disadvantages of travelling by coach does the speaker give?

    c   How often does the coach stop?

    d   How long did the coach journey last?

Speaker 4

    a   At what time of day did the speaker depart?

    b   Where did the bad smell come from?

    c   Why was the speaker able to stand outside on the deck?

    d   What was the weather like?

    e   What noises does the speaker mention?

9   Compare your answers with your partner's. Do you agree?

10 How much can you remember? With your partner, copy and complete the table of information below (not all the gaps can be filled).

	SPEAKER 1	SPEAKER 2	SPEAKER 3	SPEAKER 4
Departure time	8.30 am			
Length of journey				
Arrival time				
Weather/time of year	beautiful summer day	sunny, May		
Speaker's feelings				totally alone
Speaker with who?	wife & 3 children			
Cost			$275	

11 Read the transcript on page 158 and check your answers to Exercises 8 and 10.

12 Quiz! How much do you know about London? With your partner, choose the correct answer to each of the questions below.

   a How many people enter London every weekday between 7 am and 10 am?
      150,000   710,000   1,100,000

   b How many vehicles do the four bridges over the river Thames carry every day?
      150,000   1,100,000   2,800,000

   c What is the average time taken for people to get to work in London?
      25 minutes   55 minutes   95 minutes

   d What is the average speed of traffic in London?
      10 mph   20 mph   30 mph

 B # Reading

13 You are going to read quite a long article about the problem of traffic in London. The article was published in 2000. There are seven paragraphs in the article. The first paragraph is an introduction; the second one contains statistical facts about London; the third gives a politician's solution to the traffic problem. What do you think the other four paragraphs are about? Choose from this list:

   a more facts about London's traffic

   b traffic in other major cities

   c the writer's solutions to London's traffic problems

   d all of the above

14 The following words and phrases appear in the article. With your partner, decide on their meanings. Use a dictionary for help.

   a appalling (paragraph 1)   *really really bad*

   b congestion (1)

   c disincentive (1)

   d revive (3)

   e restricted (4)

   f road contractors (4)

   g quote (4)

   h initiatives (4)

   i traffic arteries (5)

   j radical (6)

   k seizing up (7)   *turn up*

   l implications (7)

15 Scan the article and check your answers to the quiz in Exercise 12 and the words in Exercise 14. Remember that it is not important to understand everything in the text.

Liberating London

How much longer will we have to put up with the appalling traffic in central London? This is not just a parochial concern. London is one of the three biggest cities in the world and is the motor of the British economy. Congestion is now the biggest disincentive to doing business there. Solving the congestion problem may increase the cost of living or working in London, but if nothing is done the city will slowly lose its pull.

Here are some facts. Last year 1.1 million people entered London on a typical weekday between 7 am and 10 am, and the number is rising. Most people come by train, bus or tube, but the four Thames bridges, Blackfriars, Southwark, London Bridge and Tower Bridge, together carry over 150,000 vehicles a day. The average travel time for people to get to work in central London in 1998 was 55 minutes, more than twice as long as the national average of 25 minutes. The average traffic speed in central London is about 10 mph, and it has been slowing since the 1960s. Car journeys that begin and end in central London take nearly twice as long, on average, as those by bicycle.

Ken Livingstone (the mayor of London) says that he will revive public transport and introduce congestion charges for central London. This, he claims, will reduce road traffic by 15 per cent by 2010. But a congestion tax may not survive a legal challenge and, in any case, there are more effective means to improve traffic flow. Consider these ideas.

Delivery vehicles of any kind for central London should be restricted to between 7 pm and 7 am. Some zones of European cities have adopted this idea, which obliges shops, hotels and restaurants to have staff available to take deliveries between set times. Similarly, road contractors for central London should be asked to quote for weekend and night work, particularly in office and shop areas. Both initiatives would increase costs a small amount for some businesses, but the benefits would be big.

There should also be much better coordination of roadworks between local authorities and the gas, telecom, cable-laying and other services which seem to disrupt our main traffic arteries. Penalties must be imposed for late completion of jobs. London is currently awash with roadworks and, as frustrated drivers know only too well, whole sections of road are often blocked off without any sign of work going on. There are also too many absurd cases of contractors refusing to cooperate – for example, digging up exactly the same stretch of road within days of one another. A high-profile congestion watchdog should be established as part of the Greater London Authority with an easy-to-remember telephone number which people can ring to report any unauthorised cause of congestion.

In the longer run, we may have to consider even more radical measures, such as restricting the use of cars in and out of central London to those who live there. Each London household would be allocated a permit for the use of one car only. No other cars would be allowed in. Imagine London roads without heavy traffic. It would mean a quality of urban life that Londoners can now only dream about.

Public transport would have to fill the gap created by the restriction on car use. If it cannot do so, we would need to consider huge 'park and ride' schemes around London's perimeter. The authorities in London will have to do something radical over the next 20 years to stop the city from seizing up. Such policies have important implications, and the authorities need to think boldly about them now. They can start by issuing a consultative 'green' paper to prepare Londoners for the changes ahead. For centuries London has been a planners' nightmare, but if these ideas work, it could become a model for congested cities around the world.

Source: *Prospect*, July 2000

16 Scan the article again and decide which of these ideas for improving the traffic situation in London is *not* mentioned in the text.

a banning all cars from central London

b improving public transport

c restricting delivery vehicles

d penalising contractors for not completing work on time

e restricting the use of cars to people who live in central London

C Language focus: modal verbs

17 Look at these phrases taken from the newspaper article you have read:

a Delivery vehicles of any kind for central London <u>should</u> be restricted ...

b Both initiatives <u>would</u> increase costs ...

c Penalties <u>must</u> be imposed ...

d we <u>may</u> have to consider ...

e The authorities in London <u>will</u> have to do something ...

f London ... <u>could</u> become a model for ...

In each phrase, the modal verb is underlined. What other modal verbs can you remember? Make a list.

18 What time is being referred to in each of the phrases in Exercise 18? Past? Present? Future? General time?

19 What do you notice about the word which follows each modal verb? Complete the rule for modal verbs for present/future situations:

modal verb + ...

20 Complete this rule for modal verbs for past situations:

modal verb + ... + ...

21 Complete each sentence with an appropriate modal verb and the correct form of the main verb given.

a   We ...... (go) to London by train, but I prefer the bus – it's so much cheaper.

b   She ...... (arrive) at six o'clock, but there were roadworks and terrible traffic jams which delayed her until eight.

c   You ...... (win) $500 if you have the winning ticket.

d   When we went on holiday last year, we ...... (have) a great time, but it was a disaster from start to finish.

e   You ...... (park) here – those people won't be able to get out.

f   What do you think? ...... we (meet) a little bit earlier?

g   ...... they (not think) about the problems in London years ago? It seems a bit late to start worrying now.

 D Speaking

22 Were you surprised by the facts about traffic in London in the article? What surprised you the most? How do these figures compare with your town? If you don't know, how would you go about finding out?

23 Which of the writer's suggestions is the best solution to the traffic problem in London? Why? Should all the suggestions be implemented?

24 Since this article was written (in 2000), a radical plan has been introduced in London in order to help with the traffic problem. Go to this website and find out more: http://www.cclondon.com/

25 Does your town or a town that you know have a traffic problem? If so, what is being done to overcome the problem? What would you do if you were given the responsibility for solving traffic problems? Would you use the same solution as the one introduced in London?

E **Listening**

26 Look at these **exam-type questions**. They are similar to the type you will see in Part 1 of the IGCSE Listening paper.

---

1 Marina calls her local college to get some information about evening classes. What course does Marina want to follow?

2 Gregory is telephoning a music store to order a CD. What is the order number?

3 Jeremy is trying to arrange for his cousin Melanie to come to visit him. When is she **un**able to stay?

4 You are planning a day trip in two days' time. What will the weather be like **throughout** the day? Give **two** aspects.

5 You and your friend play badminton at your local sports centre. How much does it cost for members to book a court on a weekday evening?

6 Michael wants to go to an exhibition which he has seen advertised in the newspaper and is asking someone for details. From where can he buy tickets?

---

27 With your partner, decide what information each question requires you to listen for. For example, in question 1, you need to listen for a course or a subject of study.

28 Here are the answers to some questions. Which of these answers could fit the questions above? Why?

a	tennis and football	i	3.30 pm
b	the booking office	j	£9.50
c	12 to 15 August	k	436 JWQ 9HM3
d	at the airport	l	after the traffic lights
e	Saturday 1 May	m	blue, green and white
f	photography exhibition	n	Discount Music Store
g	cloudy but warm	o	on the radio
h	English literature		

29 Listen and answer the questions in Exercise 26.

30 Compare your work with your partner's. Then read the transcript on pages 158–159 to check your answers.

! EXAM TIP

In Part 1 of the Listening paper, you hear a series of short spoken items. The sentences are not connected. For each item, you answer one question as briefly as possible, often with just one or two words. In the other parts of the Listening paper, you hear continuous, connected speech, and the questions may require you to complete a table of information, or complete some notes, or answer individual questions with short responses.

! EXAM TIP

In the exam you will be given time to read the questions before you hear the cassette/CD. Make sure you use this time well. Read all the questions and underline the key word/s in each one. Decide what type of information each question requires, for example, a number, a place, a street name.

ⓕ Further practice

31 Look at the newspaper article about activities for children: 'What to do this weekend in London'. Which activity or activities would be suitable for a family which:

a enjoys music, dance and drama from the Far East?

b likes competitions?

c would like to watch a clown?

d is only free after 6 pm?

e is interested in environmental issues?

f would like to know more about a children's television programme?

g does not want to have to buy a ticket?

WHAT TO DO THIS WEEKEND IN LONDON

Beach Camp
Walpole Park, Mattock Lane, Ealing, W5 (020-8579 5436) today and tomorrow (and until Thurs), 12 noon–6 pm, children £5, adults free.

Spend a day at the seaside without having to travel out of London. This children's event is part of Ealing's Summer Festival, and there's the added bonus that if it rains you don't have to pack up and go home either, as the 'beach' will be in a weatherproof tent.

There's also end-of-pier shows, a funfair and numerous workshops and competitions.

Hello There! The Blue Peter Experience
BBC Experience, Broadcasting House, Portland Place, W1 (0870-603 0304), today and tomorrow, 10 am–6 pm, adults £7.50, children £4.95.

The show may be over for the summer but now, with this new exhibition, young fans can find out about life behind the scenes on the long-running children's programme. There's the chance to have a go at presenting the show, watch clips of some of the most hilarious moments (that elephant is bound to be in there somewhere), as well as discovering endless fascinating facts about the programme.

Out of Asia
Victoria Embankment Gardens, Villiers St, WC2 (020-7375 0441) today and tomorrow, 2 pm–6 pm, free.

This family event celebrates the music, dance and drama of India, China and Bangladesh. For more free entertainment, head across the bridge to the National Theatre, which has a programme of outdoor events today. There's Woza Africa – a truly outstanding line-up of African music, dance and activities – at Gabriel's Wharf tomorrow.

Nikki Spencer

... AND BEYOND

Children's Festival
Cardiff Castle, Cardiff (02920 394040) today, 10.30 am–5 pm, tickets £2 (under-3s free).

It's that time of year again, when the green of Cardiff Castle is turned into a children's wonderland. This year, there's an environmental theme, so there are giant junk sculptures and a life-size whale, as well as clowns, mazes, workshops, videos and interactive exhibits.

Tomorrow for the first time ever, there's also Youth 2K, a youth arts event from 3 pm–10.30 pm (02920 873936) with everything from body art to DJs and dance ((tickets £2).

Inflatable day
Southgate Playing Fields, Crawley (01293 553636) tomorrow, 1 pm–5 pm, adults £8, children £5, family £15.

Inflatables of all shapes and sizes including giant crazy cottages, a massive pirate ship and numerous bouncy castles, mazes and bungee runs are on offer at this special event tomorrow. Other attractions include clown shows, gladiator games and Punch and Judy.

Firework Fantasia
Cannon Hill Park, Birmingham (0121-464 2000) tonight, 7 pm, adults £5, children £3 (pre-booked group ticket £10).

Pack your picnic basket for an evening of music in one of Birmingham's loveliest parks.

The concert by the City of Birmingham Symphony Orchestra will end with a fireworks display.

Source: www.visitLondon.com

Track 3

32 Listen to a short radio talk about tourist attractions in Britain. Before you listen, read the questions and decide what information is required in each answer. Then listen and write the answers to the questions.

a How much do guided tours of Canterbury Cathedral cost?

b How many attractions receive only one star for quality?

c What does Hampton Court score top marks for?

d What is Jane Ingman's least favourite attraction?

e Where is the guide to tourist attractions available from?

33 Look back at the list of advantages and disadvantages you made in Exercise 4. Choose three or four of the transport methods and write up your notes into a short paragraph of about 100 words.

34 What new attraction would you like to have in your town? Prepare a short talk outlining your ideas and giving your reasons. Be prepared to answer questions from your classmates and teacher.

Unit 5: *Exam practice*

In this unit you will have the opportunity to do some examination practice with exam-type questions. These will focus on the examination areas covered in the previous four units: exam Exercises 1 and 2 (reading), 6 and 7 (writing), and listening (Part 1).

Remember:

*for **reading** you are being assessed on:*
- *understanding and responding to information presented in a variety of forms*
- *inferring information from texts (Extended option only)*

*for **writing** you are being assessed on:*
- *communicating clearly, accurately and appropriately*
- *conveying information and expressing opinions effectively*
- *employing and controlling a variety of grammatical structures*
- *demonstrating knowledge and understanding of a range of appropriate vocabulary*
- *observing conventions of paragraphing, punctuation and spelling*
- *employing appropriate register/style*

*for **listening** you are being assessed on:*
- *understanding and responding to information presented in a variety of forms*
- *recognising, understanding and distinguishing between facts, ideas and opinions*
- *selecting and organising material relevant to specific purposes*
- *inferring information from texts (Extended option only)*

 ## Reading: Exam exercise 1

1   Read the following advertisement and answer the questions which follow.

The E-Scoot Rechargeable Battery-Operated Electric Scooter

ONLY £79.95 inc. p&p for beating traffic or just having fun!

This new, ultra-lightweight (just 7.35 kg), folding electric scooter can be great fun for all the family (minimum recommended age 10 years) – and you don't need a licence to use it.

Its rechargeable on-board batteries built in under the floor will provide power to the engine up to a maximum distance of 15 kilometres and at a maximum speed of 12 km/h. Each full charge of the batteries takes approximately 4–5 hours using the AC/DC charger provided.

The E-Scoot incorporates a foot safety cut-off switch as well as handlebar brakes. There's even a built-in stand to avoid having to lean it up against something when not in use.

E-Scoot is available in a choice of three great colours (blue, red and yellow), requires virtually no maintenance, can be used without battery power if and when required, and is available at only £79.95 each including postage and packing.

Source: Adapted from an advertisement in *The Independent on Sunday*, 8 June 2003

a How much extra do you need to pay for postage and packing? **[1]**
  None

b What can the scooter be used for? **[1]**
  beating traffic or just having fun

c Who should not use the scooter? **[1]**
  under 10 years old

d Where are the batteries located? **[1]**
  under the floor

e How far can you travel on the scooter? **[1]**
  15 km

f How long do you need to wait for the batteries to recharge? **[1]**
  4 - 5 hrs

E g In what **two** ways can the scooter be stopped? **[1]**
  battery cut off switch and handle breaks

E h What can you do if the battery runs out of power? **[1]**
  can be used without power

[Total: 8 Extended, 6 Core]

2 Read the text and answer the questions which follow.

Somewhere for the weekend ... Bilbao

This artistic city celebrates its heritage with a flamboyant fiesta, set amidst Spain's most dramatic new architecture.

Now is the time to head south-west to see Bilbao at its most active as celebrations of the city's heritage reach a climax with the Aste Nagusia festival. This is one of Spain's liveliest fiestas comprising eight days and nights of processions, parades, concerts, dances, demonstrations of rural sports (including stone lifting, log chopping and hay-bale tossing) and bullfights. There are also nightly firework displays, best viewed from the city's bridges. Bus stops and street crossings are repainted gaudily,

and bright scarves are draped around the necks of the city's statues.

Bilbao was founded in 1300 and is Spain's fourth biggest city (after Madrid, Barcelona and Valencia). Straddling the Nervion river, it is Spain's largest port. There are two official languages, Spanish and Euskara (the Basque language): most signs are bilingual.

The main tourist office is at Calle Rodrigo Arias (www.bilbao.net). It opens 9 am–2 pm and 4–7.30 pm from Monday to Friday. On Saturdays, the hours are 9 am–2 pm, on Sundays 10 am–4 pm. A more useful operation is run at the airport

(daily 7.30 am–11 pm). There is also a tourist office at the Guggenheim Museum at Avenida Abandoibarra 2, open 10 am–3 pm and 4–7 pm daily, though not on Sunday afternoons.

Many visitors and locals forsake sit-down meals in favour of nibbling at bars. Eating is no trivial matter, however. In the evenings restaurants rarely open before 9 pm. Traditional dishes revolve around veal, lamb, and fresh fish (especially cod), often in olive oil sauces.

Source: Adapted from an article in *The Independent Review*, 20 August 2003

a Why is now a good time to visit Bilbao? **[1]**
  most active as celebration

b How long do the celebrations last? *eight days and nights* **[1]**

c Give **three** examples of non-urban sports. *stone lifting, log chopping* **[1]**
  hay- bale tossing

d In what **two** ways is the city of Bilbao decorated during the fiesta? **[2]**

e Where in Spain is Bilbao situated? **[1]**

E f How many of the tourist offices are open on Sunday afternoons? **[1]**

E g How important is eating in Bilbao? **[1]**

[Total: 8 Extended, 6 Core]

Reading: Exam exercise 2 (Extended question)

3   The following article is about how a school library should be organised. Read it carefully and answer the questions which follow.

Planning and running a school library

Issuing resources manually

In order to borrow books and other materials, all users need a library card. The librarian can obtain a list of staff and pupils from the school office or personnel department in order to prepare library cards.

The normal length of borrowing depends on the person running the library, but two weeks is the suggested period of loan. The book to be borrowed is stamped two weeks in advance. The catalogue card is removed from the book, placed inside the reader ticket, and the tickets are then filed alphabetically in trays displaying the due back date. Readers can renew any resource if not requested by another user.

Usually, fines are set if users fail to return items on or before the due date. The librarian sets the fines if chosen to do so.

Some items such as videos or reference-related materials might be borrowed on an overnight loan; again, libraries can set the rules on how resources may be borrowed.

Issuing resources using an automated system

Details of all pupils and staff using the library are imported on the system. Any additions can be entered in the 'borrower' record field. All users are issued with a library ticket. These may be made manually. The following suggestions may be helpful in producing library tickets for your school:

*   The tickets could be designed by the students (as a competition) and copied.
*   The school logo and the name of the school should be included.
*   The tickets should be colour copied or just photocopied onto card. You should be able to get at least 8 tickets per sheet of card. The tickets can then be cut and barcoded.
*   Write the users' names on the tickets.
*   Go to the borrower records on the system. Find the borrower's name and scan in the barcode to register the user.
*   When all the borrowers have been registered, the library tickets can be laminated or put into plastic wallets.

Alternatively, there are reputable companies who produce library cards for schools and other organisations tailored to the purchaser's needs. Although these may work out more costly, the cards are more durable, and reduce valuable librarian time.

When a resource is loaned, the barcode on the ticket is scanned, which brings up a screen with the borrower details; the barcode on the resource is then scanned, thus recording the loan. Due back dates can be set within the system.

Maintaining resources in good condition

Resources should be kept clean and any minor repairs dealt with immediately. All paperbacks should be covered with either a plastic jacket or plastic covering. This prolongs the life of the books, especially when heavily borrowed, and the cover can be easily cleaned. Avoid using sticky tape on any resource; instead use recommended book tape for carrying out any maintenance or minor repairs on books as sticky tape can cause damage.

An annual check of all stock is recommended in order to ascertain missing resources, resources in need of repair, and resources to be withdrawn from stock. The latter may be necessary due to lack of use or because the resource has been damaged beyond repair; alternatively, the information contained within the resource may have gone out of date or have become culturally insensitive.

Source: Adapted from *Planning and Running a School Library*, University of Cambridge International Examinations, June 2002

a   What must a user have in order to borrow something from the library?   **[1]**
library card

b   How can the librarian know who needs a library card?   **[1]**
They can obtain a list of staff and pupils from school office or personnel department

c   What **two** things happen to the catalogue card after it is taken out of the book?   **[2]**
tickets are filed alphabetically in trays and displaying the due back date.

d   When is it **not** possible to renew a book?   **[1]**
if it is requested by another user

e   Give **four** pieces of advice about the design of library tickets.   **[2]**
school logo name of school included

f   What are the advantages and disadvantage in buying ready-made library cards?   **[2]**
work out cost more

g   Why should sticky tape not be used on books?   **[1]**
it can cause damage

h   Based on what you have read, make a list of **four** reasons why a resource may need to be removed from a school library.   **[4]**
lack of use
information out of date and culturally insensitive

[Total: 14]

Writing: Exam exercise 6 or 7

1   You have recently been on holiday. Write a letter to a friend or someone in your family, telling him or her about your holiday. In your letter you should:

   • explain where you went on holiday and the people who went with you

   • say what you did on holiday and whether or not you enjoyed yourself

   • say if you would recommend this type of holiday

   Your letter should be 150–200 words long (100–150 for the Core curriculum).

2   You recently went to see a film at the new cinema in your home town. Write a letter to the manager of the cinema explaining why you were dissatisfied with the facilities at the new cinema, and asking for your ticket money to be refunded. Your letter should be between 150 and 200 words long.

3   You have won a scholarship to study abroad for a year. Write a letter of between 150 and 200 words telling a member of your family about it. In your letter you should explain:

   • where you will go to study and why

   • what you are most looking forward to doing

   • the advantages this year abroad will bring

Listening: Part 1

Track 4

For questions 1–6 you will hear a series of short sentences. You will hear each item twice. Your answers should be as brief as possible.

1   Yu Ming is in his local bookshop. Where can he find a selection of dictionaries for language learners?   [1]

2   Neeta wants to book a tennis court at her local sports centre. How much does she have to pay?   [1]

3   Give **two** details about the Star Cinema.   [1]

4   Olavi is planning a trip to the beach tomorrow. What will the weather be like in the afternoon?   [1]

5   You have gone to your local shopping centre to buy a CD but the one you want is not available. How long will you have to wait before this shop can get you the CD **and** what alternative does the shop assistant offer you?   [1]

6   Daniela wants to buy a city map. Which is the best place, **and** why?   [2]

[Total: 7]

Unit 6: Focus on reading skills

Exam Exercise 2
In this unit we will concentrate on more detailed comprehension of longer texts, similar to the type to be found in Exercise 2 of the IGCSE Reading and Writing paper.

A Reading

1 You have decided to attend a course at a language school to improve your English. What facilities and services would you expect the school to have? Make a list with your partner.

FACILITIES	SERVICES
library	careers guidance

2 Which of the facilities and services on your list are the most important for you? Why?

3 The following words and phrases appear in the text you are going to read, which is taken from a brochure for a UK language school: BEET Language Centre. Discuss them with your partner and try to agree on their meanings. Use your dictionary for help.

a multi-media

b equipped with

c volumes

d on loan

e counselling

f appropriate career

g school policy

h self-catering

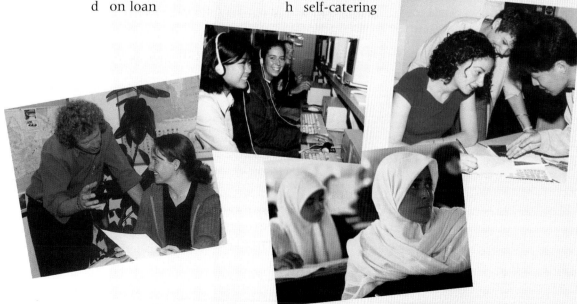

BEET Language Centre – facilities and services

Two computer centres
- 30 multi-media computers
- Free internet access all day (ADSL connection)
- 6 AAC language laboratory units

All 30 computers are equipped with CD-ROM, headphones and microphones. There is a wide range of interactive CDs for both class use and self-study. Once a week, there is normally a timetabled lesson in one of the centres. Otherwise, the centres are open for general use and for further practice of what has been learned in the classroom, and there is always someone available to help and advise you. Both centres are open from 0800. The language laboratory units offer you the following areas to choose from:

pronunciation, listening skills, grammatical exercises, and examination practice materials.

Library and bookshop
- 4000-book collection
- Cassettes, cassette players, videos
- Librarian to advise and help

The library is available to students and teacher trainees and contains about 4000 volumes. Books are graded from near-beginner to advanced level, with a good selection of books in the original version.

There is also a comprehensive collection of books for teachers and trainees. Many books come with audio-cassettes for use in the language laboratory units. However, if you wish to listen to cassettes at home, audio-cassette players are available on loan. The librarian can advise you on what materials are best for your level. You may also purchase books, at a discounted price, from the bookshop. Please note that coursebooks are included in the fees, and are yours to keep.

University Counselling Service
- Two university counsellors
- Computerised course locator
- Computerised careers guidance
- Free placement service

BEET offers free career guidance, counselling and university placement. We use the latest technology both to identify an appropriate career path and to locate a course suitable for your needs and abilities.

Cafeteria
- Meals, snacks and drinks
- Newspapers, magazines
- Open all day

The cafeteria offers hot meals, snacks, sandwiches, hot and cold drinks, fruit and chocolate. It is school policy to keep meal prices as low as possible. Generally a hot meal will cost less than half the price of a meal elsewhere. Daily newspapers and magazines are provided.

Social and leisure programme
- Free evening lectures on British culture
- Free evening activities, music, comedy theatre, etc.
- Regular Saturday excursions

BEET offers a full and varied programme of evening activities, plus regular Saturday excursions.

Accommodation
- Homestay
- Student houses (self-catering)
- Two full-time welfare officers

BEET offers year-round accommodation, either in homestay or in self-catering student houses. Most accommodation is within easy walking distance of the school.

Source: BEET Language Centre

---

4 Skim the text. What facilities and services are offered by the school? Are any of them the same as the ones you listed in Exercise 1? Are there any facilities that you would like to add? Why/Why not?

5 Look at the text again. Find the words from Exercise 3. Do the meanings you agreed on make sense?

6 Here are the answers to ten questions based on the text. Write the questions. Compare your questions with your partner's. Are they the same?

a It's free. *How much is the internet access cost*

b Once a week. *How often is there a timetabled lesson in the computer centre*

c Pronunciation, listening skills, grammatical exercises, and examination practice materials. *What is an offer can you get in language laboratory*

d About 4000.

e Audio-cassettes. *What do*

f From the bookshop.

g The latest technology.

h Daily newspapers and magazines.

i On Saturday.

j Within walking distance of the school.

B Language focus: prefixes

> Look at these phrases from the text:
> – 30 <u>multi</u>-media computers
> – Free <u>inter</u>net access all day
>
> The underlined words are **prefixes**. What is their function? Find more examples in the text.

7 With your partner, write down a definition for each of these prefixes taken from the text. Think of words beginning with each of the prefixes.

PREFIX	DEFINITION/S	WORD/S
self-	personaility	self defence
multi-	more then one	multiple choice
inter-	between, connecting	interception
con-	with	convection
micro-	very small, on a small scale	microchip
audio-	hearing, sound	audiovisual
dis-	negative	displacement
pro-		professional

8 Match each prefix below with one of the words or word stems given. Then write down the new words. What do the new words mean?

PREFIX	WORD/STEM	NEW WORD	MEANING
auto-	marine	automatic	without human control
hyper-	distant	hypermarket	
sub-	annual	submarine	below
trans-	dote	transcontinental	
equi-	president	equidistant	
bi-	matic	biannual	everyother year
mono-	diction	monolingual	
anti-	lingual	antidote	
ex-	market	president	
contra-	continental	contradiction	

C Speaking: telephone skills

9   You are going to act out a telephone conversation with your partner. Read the instructions for Student A or Student B below – your teacher will tell you which role is yours. Then, join up with some other students who have the same role, and discuss the type of language you will use during the telephone conversation. Write down your ideas.

STUDENT A	STUDENT B
I'm phoning to enquire/ask about ...	Can I help you?
How much is the ...?	What is your level of ...?

10 When you are ready, join up with a student playing the other role, and act out the telephone conversation, using the guidelines below:

Student A: You are thinking seriously about going to study English in the UK for three weeks in August, but you would like more information about some things and have decided to telephone BEET Language Centre in Bournemouth. Before you telephone, think about the information you need, and the questions you will ask. Write down the information you receive on the course dates and fees leaflet on page 45.

- the registration fee

- the number of lessons and evening lectures on the courses

- the weekly fees for the courses

- the cost of accommodation in both homestay and student house

- start and finish dates in August

- the cost of a transfer

Student B: You work at BEET Language Centre in Bournemouth. Answer your partner's questions using the course dates and fees leaflet on page 46. You will need to obtain your partner's details for the enrolment form. Before you write anything, think about the information you need, and the questions you will ask. Use the enrolment form on page 47 to help you prepare your questions about:

- personal details (name, address, etc.)

- level of English

- course required

- travel and transfer details

BEET
LANGUAGE CENTRE

Nortoft Road, Charminster
Bournemouth BH8 8PY, ENGLAND
Tel: +44 1202 397721
Fax: +44 1202 309662
E-mail: admin@beet.co.uk
Website: http://www.beet.co.uk

COURSE DATES & FEES

REGISTRATION FEE

Payable once only on enrolment	£_____ (1)

MAIN COURSES, INTENSIVE AND EXTRA INTENSIVE – ALL YEAR

Course	Code	Lessons per week	Fees per week
Main	B	(2) _____ lessons General English + 2 Evening Lectures	(3) £ _____
Intensive	A	20 lessons General English + (4) _____ lessons Options Programme + 2 Evening Lectures	(5) £ _____
Extra Intensive	AA	20 lessons General English + 8 lessons Options Programme + (6) _____ Evening Lectures	(7) £ _____

Month	Start on one of these dates	Finish on one of these dates
January	5, 19	16, 30
February	2, 16*	13, 27
March	1, 15*, 29	12, 26
April	13*, 26	8, 23
May	10*, 24	7, 21
June	7*, 21	4, 18
July	(8) _____	(9) _____
August	2, 16, 31	13, 27
September	13, 27	10, 24
October	11*, 25	8, 22
November	8*, 22*	5, 19
December		17

* Not Beginner or Elementary Levels

ACCOMMODATION (HOMESTAY OR STUDENT HOUSE)

Homestay and Private Home	Costs per Week	Homestay only: A weekly retention fee of £30 is payable if you wish to keep the room whilst away, for example on holiday	IMPORTANT Please read Notes 3 and 4(a) below
Single room (all year, except July and August)	£75		
Single room (July 3 to August 28 only)	(10) £_____		
Shared room (all year)	(11) £_____		
Christmas and New Year Holiday Supplement	£26 (Xmas week only)		

Student House (Self-Catering Residence)		The minimum age for living in a Student House is (12) _____ years	IMPORTANT Please read Note 4(b) below
Single room	£85		
Twin or Double room	£70 per person		

Transfer Prices (one-way)

From: Heathrow Airport: (13) _____
    Gatwick Airport: £95
    (14) _____: £118

NB. These are prices for the cost of a one-way transfer by private car. When there are 2–4 students, the cost will be shared equally. Airport transfers must be paid for in full in advance. Part-refunds, where applicable, will be made in England.

BEET
LANGUAGE CENTRE

Nortoft Road, Charminster
Bournemouth BH8 8PY, ENGLAND
Tel: +44 1202 397721
Fax: +44 1202 309662
E-mail: admin@beet.co.uk
Website: http://www.beet.co.uk

COURSE DATES & FEES

REGISTRATION FEE

Payable once only on enrolment	£65

MAIN COURSES, INTENSIVE AND EXTRA INTENSIVE – ALL YEAR

Course	Code	Lessons per week	Fees per week
Main	B	20 lessons General English + 2 Evening Lectures	£155
Intensive	A	20 lessons General English + 4 lessons Options Programme + 2 Evening Lectures	£175
Extra Intensive	AA	20 lessons General English + 8 lessons Options Programme + 2 Evening Lectures	£190

Month	Start on one of these dates	Finish on one of these dates
January	5, 19	16, 30
February	2, 16*	13, 27
March	1, 15*, 29	12, 26
April	13*, 26	8, 23
May	10*, 24	7, 21
June	7*, 21	4, 18
July	5, 19	2, 16, 30
August	2, 16, 31	13, 27
September	13, 27	10, 24
October	11*, 25	8, 22
November	8*, 22*	5, 19
December		17

* Not Beginner or Elementary Levels

ACCOMMODATION (HOMESTAY OR STUDENT HOUSE)

Homestay and Private Home	Costs per Week	Homestay only: A weekly retention fee of £30 is payable if you wish to keep the room whilst away, for example on holiday	**IMPORTANT** Please read Notes 3 and 4(a) below
Single room (all year, except July and August)	£75		
Single room (July 3 to August 28 only)	£86		
Shared room (all year)	£65		
Christmas and New Year Holiday Supplement	£26 (Xmas week only)		
Student House (Self-Catering Residence)		The minimum age for living in a Student House is 18 years	**IMPORTANT** Please read Note 4(b) below
Single room	£85		
Twin or Double room	£70 per person		

Transfer Prices (one-way)
From: Heathrow Airport: £80
     Gatwick Airport: £95
     Central London: £118

NB. These are prices for the cost of a one-way transfer by private car. When there are 2–4 students, the cost will be shared equally. Airport transfers must be paid for in full in advance. Part-refunds, where applicable, will be made in England.

BEET

ENROLMENT FORM

LANGUAGE CENTRE

Agent's Name:	Please attach 3 passport photos

1) Personal Details

Mr/Mrs/Miss/Ms: .... Given Name(s): ....

Family Name(s): ....

Address: ....

....

Tel: .... Fax: .... Email: ....

Birth Date: .... Nationality: ....

Mother Tongue(s): ....

Profession: ....

How do you know about BEET? ....

Level of English	Please tick ✓		
Beginner	☐	Intermediate	☐
Near Beginner	☐	Upper Intermediate	☐
Elementary	☐	Advanced	☐
Lower Intermediate	☐	Very Advanced	☐

2) Course Details

Course Name	Course Code	Start Date (day / month / year)	Finish Date (day / month / year)	Number of Weeks

Options Programme (Intensive Courses only) Please list the options you would like to study, if known	Examinations Please list the examinations you would like to take, if known

3) Travel Details

Do you want an airport transfer? (Please tick ✓): ☐ Yes ☐ No

Airport: ....

Flight Number: ....

Arrival Date (day / month / year): ....

Arrival Time: ....

Office Use only
Name: ....
Address: ....
....
Tel: ....

D Speaking: giving advice

11 Here is the beginning of a magazine article you are going to read:

Changing schools – a survival guide for students and parents

The first day at a new school can be worrying for both parents and children.

Read on to discover how to prepare for the big day …

Why do you think that 'The first day at a new school can be worrying for both parents and children'? Think back to when you started your current school. What was it like? What worries (if any) did you have? How did you deal with them? How much support did you get from your friends and family? What did you do in order 'to prepare for the big day'?

12 What advice could you give to someone who is about to change schools? With your partner, think about the type of language you could use, and make a list of phrases.

ADVICE PHRASES
If I were you I'd/I wouldn't …
It might be a good idea to …

13 Work with a different partner. Give each other some advice in preparation for a change of schools. Try to use the advice phrases from Exercise 12, and your ideas from Exercise 11.

Example: If I were you I'd try to visit the school as much as possible before your first day.

E Reading

14 Look at these words and phrases which have been removed from the article. With your partner, quickly discuss the meanings. Use your dictionary for help.

   a 'rights' and 'wrongs'   f responsibility

   b bullying   g significant transition

   c involvement   h stability

   d plunged into   i traumatic

   e potential problems

15 Quickly read the text. Do not worry about the gaps at the moment. As you read, think about your responses in Exercise 11. Are there any similarities?

Changing schools – a survival guide for students and parents

The first day at a new school can be worrying for both parents and children. Read on to discover how to prepare for the big day …

Secondary school

Going to secondary or high school marks a (1) from childhood to becoming a teenager. For children, it is about leaving the security of primary school and being (2) a new and unknown environment; and for adults, the move from primary school shows that a child is growing up.

Preparation

Parents probably have all kinds of worries, but they are often totally unaware of the problems that teenagers may face. According to a recent survey, 42 per cent of parents thought that drugs were the biggest problem for their teenage children, but only 19 per cent of teenagers themselves were worried about drugs. The biggest worry for teens is their relationships with friends, closely followed by (3).

When children leave primary school, parents usually have less (4) with the new secondary school and with their child's education. Teenagers often make their own way to and from school, so parents no longer have the opportunity to meet each other while waiting for their children to finish school for the day. Parents' communication with secondary school is frequently through the child, rather than through direct involvement with the teachers.

Being prepared for the change from primary to secondary school can help to dispel any fears. Here are some useful tips:

- Talking about what to expect is often very helpful – it is not necessary to find solutions to (5), but talking about things can help teenagers to cope with their own feelings about going to a new school.
- Staying with friends who have come with them from primary school will discourage other children from bullying. Obviously teenagers will soon make new friends in their new school, but it is important to have the (6) of old friends, at least for a while. For those children who have few or no friends, it is important that they quickly make friends with other children of their own age and interests.
- Fitting in is very important at this age. Parents need to find out what other teenagers are doing so that their kid does not feel left out. Wearing the wrong sweatshirt, having the wrong type of school bag, or even arriving at school at the wrong time, can all be very (7) for any teenager.

College

In many ways, moving on to college is the least traumatic school change that someone has to face. Often, college is simply a continuation of secondary or high school in the same building; however, for others, it may mean yet another move to a different school in a different part of town, or even in a completely different town or city. But college provides an opportunity for a teenager to mature, gain more independence, and build their confidence.

Preparation

This is an age of choices, so it is up to each individual teenager to get on with their studies. Parents can no longer enforce 'rules' as they might have done in earlier years. Whatever problems or questions a teenager may have, it is essential that parents do not lecture their children about (8). Instead, it is far more productive to encourage teenagers to talk about their own views.

Here are some useful tips:

- Teenagers need independence. Parents may have to 'let go' more than they want to, but it is very important to give teenage children their own space, and not interfere.
- Teenagers at college are nearly adults, and should not be treated like children. However, teenagers who want independence must be prepared to take (9) for their own actions.
- Parents need to support their teenagers, even though this may sometimes be difficult.

Source: Adapted from 'First day survival guide' by Sheena Miller, *in ASDA magazine*, August 2003

16 Read the text again. Put the words and phrases from Exercise 14 into the gaps. Check your answers with your partner.

17 Answer the following questions:

a Why is going to secondary school an important change for a child?

b According to the survey, what is the second most important concern for teenagers?

c Why do parents often have less direct communication with secondary schools?

d What can help to discourage bullying at school?

e Why could arriving at school at the wrong time be a worry for a teenager?

f What alternative is given to lecturing teenagers about 'rights' and 'wrongs'?

(F) Further practice

18 Write a letter to a friend or family member who is about to change schools, giving them advice on how to prepare for the change. Think about your ideas from Exercise 11 and those you read in the text 'Changing schools'. You should write 150–200 words for the Extended curriculum and 100–150 words for the Core curriculum.

19 Read the text 'Communicating with the world?' and answer the questions which follow.

   a Which levels of language are the audiomagazines suitable for?

   b What is contained in the magazine which accompanies the CD or cassette?

   c How much time is needed for improvement?

   d Where should you go for further information?

   e Which course will provide you with information about cars?

   f What would you expect Roberto Tornato's job to be?

   g What is the total cost including postage and packing for the Italian course on CD with the study supplement and video?

   h How many methods of payment are offered?

20 Look again at the text 'Communicating with the world?'. Find examples of words with prefixes. Are there any prefixes which you have not already met in this unit? Make a list and check in your dictionary if you are unsure about their meaning.

21 Write an extra paragraph of about 60 words to insert into the BEET text on page 42, describing a facility not already mentioned. Think carefully about the style and content of your paragraph.

Communicating with the world?

A foreign language could help

LanguageLearning audiomagazines have for many years helped learners of all levels to develop and improve their foreign language skills in order to communicate effectively. Available in French, Spanish, Italian and Greek (and in German from next year!), each unique edition arrives in your home or office complete with a CD or cassette, packed with 90 minutes of authentic radio and TV interviews, conversations, and news items about up-to-date current affairs, travel, entertainment, the arts, sports and health issues. As well as the CD or cassette, subscribers receive a magazine which includes a word-for-word transcript of everything, a mini-glossary, and information about the source of the listening material. An optional study supplement provides further listening comprehension practice, and an optional video provides a further source of practice material in each issue.

Each magazine is produced in a European capital: Paris, Madrid, Rome or Athens, by a team of professional language trainers working with journalists and businesspeople. You need only spend a few hours each month and you will see your vocabulary and confidence building at an amazing rate. Furthermore, your knowledge of national events and culture will increase dramatically. Visit our website to find out more and see examples of what LanguageLearning audiomagazines offer.

www.LanguageLearning.com

Bonjour! in French
This month's special features: The success of French soccer over the past five years, with interviews with the top football stars and managers. Are French chefs the best in the world? A gastronomic look at French cuisine. The merger of Renault and Nissan – what does it mean for car buyers?

¡Ola! in Spanish
Holidays in Spain – can you avoid the tourists? We check out the best places to visit. What's the most unusual job you can think of? How about clock tower repairing – this month we have a special feature on this strange but important job.

Ciao! in Italian
Traffic in Rome – a look at how the government plans to improve pollution and congestion. Ever been on a gondola in Venice and wondered how they are made? Roberto Tornato explains all! And pasta – just how many different shapes are there?

Yiassas! in Greek
The Olympics – what has Athens learned from the experience? Salonika – the 'other' part of Greece. And GreekJet, the new charter company which aims to take more than 20% of the tourist market – what does it offer the traveller?

ORDER FORM
A subscription to any of the 4 audiomagazines costs £65.00, plus an additional £12.00 if on CD. The optional study supplement and video are £15.00 and £18.00 respectively. P&P is included in the basic price. Please add £2.50 if ordering the video.

Name: ....
Address:
....
Postcode: ....
Payment by CHEQUE ☐ VISA ☐   MASTERCARD ☐ AMEX ☐
If paying by credit card, please supply:
Card number: .... Expiry date: ....
Signature: ....

For faster service, order via telephone **+44-1202-789 1234** or fax **+44-1202-789 1289** or on-line
www.LanguageLearning.com with your credit card details.
Language Learning Ltd, Europa House, Summer Lane, Epsom, Surrey KT17 1JG

Unit 7: *Focus on reading and writing skills*

Exam Exercise 4

In this unit we will concentrate on the skills needed to make notes, which you do in Exercise 4 of the IGCSE Reading and Writing paper.

> *In Exercise 4, you need to understand information presented in a variety of ways, and to select and organise material in order to complete some notes or a form. You need to communicate clearly and accurately, and in the Extended option you will also need to produce a short piece of writing.*
>
> Marks = 8 Extended, 6 Core.

Ⓐ Reading: looking for details

1   What job would you like to do when you finish your education? Have you always wanted to do this job, or have your ideas changed as you have grown older? What in particular appeals to you about this job? Are there any negative aspects to it?

2   Find five jobs hidden in the wordbox.

Q	W	E	R	U	T	Y	C	U	I
P	O	A	S	M	D	F	A	G	H
J	C	A	R	P	E	N	T	E	R
K	U	L	Z	I	X	C	E	V	B
N	R	M	P	R	O	I	R	U	Y
K	A	L	Q	E	W	E	E	R	T
J	T	H	G	V	F	X	R	D	I
A	O	H	O	E	Y	N	M	A	S
G	R	O	U	N	D	S	M	A	N

3   What does each person do? Complete each sentence with a job from Exercise 2.

   a   A ...... looks after a museum.

   b   Someone who makes things from wood is called a ......

   c   A ...... is a person who is paid to provide food and drinks at a party or meeting.

   d   A ......'s job is to take care of a large garden or sports field.

   e   Someone who controls a game of tennis is called the ......

4   You are going to read a newspaper article about a carpenter. Before you read, what do you think are the positive and negative aspects of being a carpenter?

ADVANTAGES	DISADVANTAGES
very creative	can be dangerous

5   Quickly scan the text and check if any of your ideas from Exercise 4 are in the article 'An art no more?'

An art no more?

The sound of a saw screeching through wood is deafening. Sawdust is billowing into the air and the watchful eyes of the carpenter who is sitting hunched over a menacing machine. Agile hands transfer the piece of wood to a large electronic machine and guide it into position. The sharp edges of the machine are only millimetres away from the skin of the carpenter's quick-moving fingers. A slight loss of total concentration could result in accidental amputation, but the master craftsman in question shows no fear as the wood is trimmed. As the dust-filled air begins to clear, it is possible to see the face of this highly skilled artisan. The delicate features and frame of the 60-year-old in question are in stark contrast to the stereotypical image of a carpenter.

This carpenter has perfected her craft for more than 25 years in her workshop in the middle of Nicosia, spending each day lifting and carrying large pieces of timber, using dangerous power tools and assembling any number of different timber items. As far as she is aware, this carpenter is the only professional female carpenter on the island of Cyprus.

Born in Nicosia 60 years ago, Soulla attended school until she was ten, when she left to help in her mother's dressmaking business. At the age of 17 she became engaged to a friend of ten years, Kypros, and two years later they married.

Soulla Athanasiou learned the art of carpentry from her husband, and as a result of his careful tutoring, she says that she can make absolutely anything, although she mostly enjoys making furniture because she likes to see the finished product. She also enjoys making smaller items such as backgammon boards and drinks trays with unique designs and patterns, using delicate tools and techniques.

Despite the obvious dangers of working with power tools, the long-term effect on Soulla's health gives her more cause for concern. She has problems with her spine and with the nerves in her hands, and has decided to retire soon. It is remarkable that only her back and hands are giving her trouble. Soulla spray-paints some of her finished products and the smell of the chemicals is extremely strong, although she is certain that this has not

affected her breathing and her lungs.

None of Soulla's family has followed in her footsteps, and she is sad that the current younger generation in Cyprus are not taking up the skills of the old craftsmen. She says that there will come a time when it will not be possible to get anything repaired.

Source: Adapted from the *Cyprus Sunday Mail*, 3 September 2000

6   Read the article again, this time in more detail. What information can you find about being a carpenter? What words and phrases in the text give you this information? Look at the examples, and then try to find and list at least five more pieces of information. Put the information into your own words where possible.

INFORMATION	WORDS AND PHRASES FROM TEXT
noisy	The sound of a saw … is deafening
dirty	Sawdust is billowing, dust-filled air

7   Compare your answers with your partner's. Did you include the same information from the text? What information is different? If you have the same information, did you also have the same words and phrases from the text?

B Writing: making notes and writing a paragraph

8 Look at the article once more and find information about Soulla Athanasiou. Which words and phrases in the text give you this information? Look at the examples, and then try to find and list at least five more pieces of information. Put the information into your own words where possible.

INFORMATION	WORDS AND PHRASES FROM TEXT
very talented	highly skilled artisan
age 60	Born ... 60 years ago, 60-year-old

9 Compare your answers with your partner's. Did you include the same information from the text? What information is different? If you have the same information, did you also have the same words and phrases from the text?

10 Imagine that you are a journalist and you are going to write an article about Soulla Athanasiou and her work. Copy and complete the notes below, using the article you have read and the information you wrote in Exercises 6 and 8.

An art no more?

Skills required:
watchful eyes
(1) ......
quick-moving fingers
(2) ......
no fear

Negative aspects of job:
(3) ...... and (4) ......
dangerous

Soulla Athanasiou:
born (5) ...... years ago in (6) ......
married at age (7) ......
learned job from her (8) ......
enjoys making furniture, (9) ......
and (10) ......
has problems with spine and (11) ...... but no
problems with (12) ......

11 Using your notes from Exercise 10, write a paragraph about Soulla Athanasiou and her work. Do not write more than about 100 words.

12 Exchange your writing with your partner. Check your partner's work. What exactly should you be looking for?

C Speaking: giving advice

13 Read this conversation between Sipho and Tendani. Copy down any phrases which give advice, for example 'if I were you …'. Compare your answers with your partner's.

Sipho: *What an amazing woman she is!*

Tendani: *She's had a very hard but interesting life, hasn't she?*

Sipho: *Yes. I just don't know what to do when I finish school after my IGCSEs.*

Tendani: *Well, if I were you, I'd think seriously about it.*

Sipho: *Why?*

Tendani: *Well, for one thing, there are so many possibilities.*

Sipho: *Yes, I know, but where do I go to find out information?*

Tendani: *You ought to speak to the careers advisor at school.*

Sipho: *I have done but she always asks me the same question: 'What do you want to do when you leave school?'!*

Tendani: *Why don't you make a list of ideas before you see her?*

Sipho: *Yes, I should, shouldn't I?*

Tendani: *What about speaking to your parents? I'm sure they could help.*

Sipho: *Yes, you're right. I'll speak to them tonight and then make a list! You know something, Tendani? You should be a careers advisor!*

14 Copy and complete the table below.

ADVICE PHRASES
Example: If I were you, I + would + infinitive
You ought to + ……
Why don't you + …… ?
What about + …… ?
You should + ……

15 Add some more advice phrases to the list in Exercise 14.

16 Think back to your ideas in Exercise 1 in this unit. Discuss them with your partner. Give each other advice about your future jobs. Try to use some of the advice phrases from Exercises 13 and 14.

17 What advice would you give to someone who was thinking of doing the following jobs? What are the advantages and disadvantages of each one? Give reasons.

a   an accountant

b   a teacher

c   a pilot

d   a doctor

e   a curator

 D   Reading

18 What do you think are the most important aspects of a job: a good salary? Long holidays? Discuss with your partner and make a list.

19 You are going to read a text introducing some of the people who work at the tennis championships played every year at Wimbledon. Before you read, match the words and phrases in the box with the jobs you found in Exercise 2 (excluding 'carpenter'). Compare your answers with your partner.

grass	museum	on court	cups of coffee
200 men and 121 women		auctions	
cover Centre Court in 28 seconds		restaurant	

THE CATERER

Frank McCartney is the director of catering for the All England Club

❝I had worked at the Championships for many years with Town and County. Then, a few summers ago, Gardner Merchant bought them out and it soon became apparent that things were not working out. So a couple of colleagues and I set up a catering company called FMC – I'm Frank, and there's also Martin and Colin. Last year was our first Wimbledon. As the only official catering company at the All England Club, we are responsible for providing everyone with food, from the ball boys to the Royal Family. We deal with up to 37,000 people a day. Out of those, we'll serve 6,000 a proper sit-down meal in a restaurant setting. With so many guests, we naturally require a vast staff, which is why we employ 1,500 over the course of the fortnight (1,474 of which are temps). The average lunch would consist of salmon or beef, although we also provide vegetarian options or nicer foods such as lobster. To give you an idea of the amounts we are talking about, we use something like two tons of salmon a day, one ton of beef, 190,000 sandwiches and 305,000 cups of coffee and tea. Naturally the players are given more high-energy produce to eat, like pasta and fruits (Pete Sampras likes his bananas), but the Royals' meals are top secret. ❞

THE CURATOR

Honor Godfrey is the new curator of the museum, to be found at Gate 4

❝I took over last October, so in a sense I have gone full circle, as I was a researcher when the museum first opened back in 1977, as part of the celebrations for the 100th All England Championships. It's really nice to be back now, because I have such a vivid memory of how the whole museum was born. There have been many changes here since then, of course, most notably the big redesign which took place in 1985 to accommodate the ever-increasing collection. In fact, the collecting never stops as we are constantly on the lookout for new things to fill our shelves. In the main, we are either given articles by members of the public or we go to specific auctions. The one other way in which we build memorabilia is thanks to the players. I have made a special plea this year, asking players, past and present, to donate anything which they think may be of interest to visitors and tennis fans. My personal favourite items are all the earlier Victorian artefacts. In particular, there is an inkwell in the shape of a tennis ball and a letter holder designed to look like a net, which I love. The trick with this job, as the previous curator demonstrated over the course of her 20-year tenure, is to put your imprint on the museum. Hopefully, I can make it my 'baby'.❞

THE UMPIRES' UMPIRE

Sultan Gangji was born in Zanzibar and is head umpire at Wimbledon

❛ I'm in charge of all the organisation and back-up for the Wimbledon umpires. I have 321 umpires (200 men and 121 women), ranging from gold badges to novices, who are selected from Britain and overseas. There are 55 chair umpires and the rest watch the lines. This year I will have 60 foreign umpires, which should create an international flavour. Once selected, they are kitted out with their personal uniform. Ages range from 16 to 66, and the average age is in the mid-40s. For the first time, we have our own headquarters on the ground floor of the Millennium Building. The main advantages are that we'll now have more space to rest, and will be given separate changing-rooms for men and women as well, something we never had before. This job is demanding but equally fulfilling. I am not just deciding who umpires where, there are also finances and training to deal with. I have to ensure I stay within budget, while retaining the highest possible quality of umpiring. We have courses throughout the winter months to give umpires a flavour of what they will be dealing with on court. Apart from teaching the basics, we also watch videos to show how arguments with players can escalate. As you can guess, John McEnroe features prominently. ❜

THE GROUNDSMAN

Eddie Seaward has been Wimbledon head groundsman since 1991

❛ My life is ruled by the date of the Championships; 25 weeks to the fortnight all too quickly become five. Then six days. Time just slips away. I feel that every year. And the closer I get to the first day, the more paranoid I get about the grass. I can walk on to Centre Court and know instinctively the state of the turf. But if I see a mark on the court on a Friday night, by Monday morning, after a weekend's worry, it's become a crater. As the Championships draw near, my life is dominated by weather forecasts. It becomes fanatical, almost destructive and you have to step back sometimes and remember you can't do anything about it. The nightmare is one of those overcast, showery days when the covers are always coming on and off and you get neck-ache looking at the sky. We can cover Centre Court in 28 seconds, but the trick is to anticipate the rain and get the covers on before it starts. I used to queue to get into Wimbledon and never dreamed I'd ever work here. The beauty of the place can still take your breath away. In the autumn the creeper turns red and the clubhouse looks magnificent. It's a magical place. The whole atmosphere, the whole feeling of it, even on cold, wet, winter days. I am privileged to work here. ❜

Source: *The Independent on Sunday*, 25 June 2000

20 Skim the texts about the people who work at Wimbledon and check your answers to Exercise 19.

21 Look at the texts in more detail and answer the following questions.

  a Which **two** people worked at Wimbledon before their present jobs?

  b Why is bad weather the groundsman's nightmare?

  c What is available for visitors to eat at Wimbledon?

  d What are the main advantages of the Millennium Building for the umpires?

  e What does the curator hope to be doing during her time at Wimbledon?

  f Give **three** ways in which the museum adds to its collection of memorabilia.

22 The Wimbledon texts include a lot of numbers and dates. What do the following numbers and dates refer to?

  Example: *37,000 = the number of people who eat each day at the All England Club*

  a 190,000   d 25 weeks

  b mid-40s   e 20-year tenure

  c 1977   f 1,474

23 Here are 11 words taken from the four Wimbledon texts. The letters of the words have been mixed up, except for the first letter. Unjumble the letters and write down the words.

TEXTS	WORDS
The caterer	tmpes vgtraeeain
The umpires' umpire	neiovcs hretrauqdaes
The curator	meoaiilbrma pale actfaters
The groundsman	piaronad truf certar atcptniiae

24 Which definition matches each of the 11 words as used in the texts? Compare your answers with your partner's.

  a appeal, request

  b centre of operations

  c large hole in the ground

  d someone who does not eat meat

  e beginners, learners

  f objects made in the past, with historical importance

  g grass

  h stand-in workers

  i things connected with a famous person or subject

  j obsessed, worried

  k forecast

E Writing: making notes and writing a paragraph

25 You are going to make some notes and write a paragraph about 'The caterer'.
First, look at these notes and the paragraph about 'The umpires' umpire'.

NOTES

Name of head umpire:	*Sultan Gangji*
Job details:	*in charge of 321 umpires from all over the world*
	decides who umpires each match
	finances, training
Information about umpires:	*200 men, 121 women*
	given personal uniforms
	ages 16–66, average mid-40s
	training courses during winter months
Umpires' headquarters:	*ground floor Millennium Building*
Advantages:	*space to relax, separate changing rooms*

PARAGRAPH

Sultan Gangji is the head umpire at Wimbledon and is in charge of 321 umpires from Britain and overseas. Apart from deciding which person umpires each match, he also organises their training and the finances. There are 200 male and 121 female umpires, aged between 16 and 66. After being selected, they are given a personal uniform, and have to attend training courses during the winter months. They have their own headquarters in the Millennium Building, where there is plenty of space and separate changing facilities for men and women.
(90 words)

26 Make notes about the 'The caterer' text and write a paragraph. Do not write more than 100 words.

Name:
Name of catering company:
Information about the company:
People served each day:
People served in restaurant:
Number of temporary and permanent staff:
Typical lunch food:
Other options available:
Amount of food and drink consumed in one day:

⑤ Further practice

27 Look at the Open University (OU) advertisement. Find and copy down the advantages of studying with the OU. Write a paragraph about the advantages. Do not write more than 100 words.

What can the Open University do for you?

We can offer you a place at one of the best universities in Britain. We'll provide you with a choice of 168 first-class courses developed especially to enable you to study in your own time, backed by the Open University's own unique study method – OU supported open learning.

We'll give you the support of a personal tutor, and the chance to meet your fellow students. You can take one-off courses, diplomas, a degree or a postgraduate degree. Subjects available include: Computing, Business Management, Technology, Modern Languages, Social Sciences, English Law, Arts, Science, Mathematics, Education and Health & Social Welfare.

Whether you want to study to improve your career prospects or for your own personal interest, there's almost certainly a course for you. If you haven't studied for a while, we'll help you get started. No previous qualifications are required, you just need a lively intelligence and a willingness to learn. It's real value for money and you can pay by monthly instalments.

Open University course materials are of the highest quality and come in a variety of forms, including video and audio tapes as well as texts. The OU leads the world in its use of new technology for learning. A number of courses provide source material on CD-ROM.

Did you know?

- *The OU is in the top 15% of all UK universities for teaching quality*
- *25% of all British MBAs come from the OU*
- *Over 30,000 employers have sponsored their staff on OU courses*
- *75,000 OU students are online from home*
- *There are 9-month courses and new diplomas as well as degrees*

Source: *The Independent on Sunday*, 4 June 2000

28 Interview someone you know about his or her job. Find out what the advantages and disadvantages of the job are, and what ambitions, if any, the person has. During the interview, make notes. Then write a paragraph of no more than 100 words.

Hi-5 Trampolines

Trampolining is great fun for all ages! It improves coordination, balance skills and spatial awareness. You could be the next Olympic champion trampolinist!

Hi-5 produces three different sizes of trampoline:

CODE #T1 trampoline
£250   300 cm diameter   max weight 80 kg
cover £13.95
anchor kit £19.95 (CODE #AK1)

CODE #T2 trampoline
£350   400 cm diameter
max weight 120 kg
cover £29.95
anchor kit £29.95
(CODE #AK2)

CODE #T3 trampoline
£580   500 cm diameter   max weight 140 kg
cover £57.95
anchor kit £39.95 (CODE #AK3)   fun ring £199.95 (CODE #FR3)

STRENGTH Hi-5 trampolines are guaranteed for ten years against rust causing damage to the 2 mm steel frames. The top and bottom rails of the frame are specially designed to give extra strength and stability; this prevents twisting and bending.

WEATHERPROOF The jumping mat is a soft but strong material held in place by steel springs. It is specially treated to protect it against the harmful rays of the sun, as well as rain. While we do not recommend that your Hi-5 trampoline is left outside in the rain, the mat is 100% weatherproof!

ACCESSORIES Three optional accessories are available for your Hi-5 trampoline. Firstly, a plastic **cover** with drainage holes for rain and an elastic rim so that it neatly fits your trampoline. There are three sizes available. Secondly, an **anchor kit** to protect your trampoline from high winds. The kit consists of four straps which attach to your trampoline and to stakes in the ground. Thirdly, a fun ring safety system for youngsters and trampoline beginners. The fun ring attaches our #T3 trampoline, providing a secure environment in which to practise and play.

When we deliver, our experts can help you to set up your new trampoline and accessories – FREE OF CHARGE!

For more information about Hi-5 trampolines and accessories, visit our website www.hi-5trampolines.com, or email us enquiries@hi-5trampolines.com

You want to order the following items from Hi-5 Trampolines:

- a trampoline for weight up to 110 kg
- equipment to protect the trampoline from high winds
- equipment to protect the trampoline from the rain

You will be at home on Wednesday, but only in the morning. You do not need help in putting the equipment together in your garden.

Copy and complete the order form in full.

Hi-5 Trampolines Order Form

FIRST NAME: _____   FAMILY NAME: _____

ADDRESS: _____

DELIVERY DAY: _____   DELIVERY TIME: _____
(MORNING OR AFTERNOON)

EQUIPMENT REQUIRED

ITEM	CODE	NAME	DIAMETER	WEIGHT	PRICE
1					
2					
3					
4					

☐ Tick the box if you do NOT require assistance in setting up your new Hi-5 trampoline and accessories.

Unit 8: *Focus on writing skills*

Exam Exercises 6 and 7
In this unit we will concentrate on the skills needed to write a formal letter, which you may be asked to do in Exercise 6 or Exercise 7 of the IGCSE E2L Reading and Writing paper. Remember that a formal letter will have a different style and format from an informal letter (see Unit 3).

Ⓐ Spelling

1   Look at this extract from the BEET text in Unit 6:

'… *the centres are open for general use and for further* <u>practice</u> *of what has been learned in the classroom, and there is always someone available to help and* <u>advise</u> *you.*'

What part of speech are the underlined words: nouns? adjectives? verbs? What do you notice about their spelling? Can you think of a spelling rule for the two underlined words, depending on what part of speech they are?

2   Some British English (BrE) words and American English (AmE) words differ in their spelling, such as 'theatre' (BrE) and 'theat<u>er</u>' (AmE). With your partner, make a list of any words you know which change their spelling in American English.

! EXAM TIP

In the IGCSE examination, it doesn't matter if you use BrE or AmE spelling, as long as you are consistent. In other words, you cannot use both!

Also, it does not matter if you speak with an accent as examiners are used to a range of accents from all over the world. You do not need to have a British English accent to get a good mark in the Speaking exam!

3   Correct the spelling mistakes in the following list of words. All the words appear in the text you are going to read. You can check your corrections later.

alltogether   sugestion   assosiation   beleive   cusin   secondery studing   univercity   increaseingly   paralel   comunication

4   Which words do you normally spell incorrectly? Can you think of a method to help you spell these words correctly? How do you keep a record of vocabulary items?

Ⓑ Reading

5   The seven words and phrases in the left-hand column appear in the text you are going to read. Match each one with a suitable definition. Be careful! There are two extra definitions which you do not need to use. Use your dictionary for help.

a	logic	i	sign an agreement
b	nuisance	ii	say goodbye
c	farewell	iii	something which annoys or causes problems
d	mayhem	iv	reasons
e	grappling with	v	confused situation

6   Here is the text, but five of the seven paragraphs are in the wrong order. With your partner, rearrange these paragraphs into the correct order. Do *not* worry about the numbered gaps at the moment.

New Zealand moves to allow spelling of choice

Paragraph A

Proposals have been put before English teachers in New Zealand to allow their students to pick and choose from the language's American and British orthographies: colour or color, program or programme, and so on. If the proposals are adopted, conventional British variants of the words could be dropped altogether, and the local version of the language as it is taught switched to the American vernacular.

Paragraph B

Many of the New Zealand teachers surveyed said that English spelling in any form was a poor cousin to imagination and creative thought on the part of students, although some remained unsure whether the time is yet right for the Kiwis to (**3**) to British English.

Paragraph C

In a syndicated column on English usage, Frank Haden, a local writer who styles himself as an Anglophile curmudgeon, predicted (**4**) in the local classrooms if either of the proposals are adopted. 'Take a deep breath,' he wrote, 'introduce American spellings, declare them the correct ones, deduct marks from any pupil who tries to smuggle through an English spelling, then stand back. Chaos will naturally follow.' In Haden's view, many of the stateside variants introduced to the language only ever happened because the Americans 'didn't know any better'. New Zealanders, he feels, do.

Paragraph D

Opinions were recently canvassed in the organisation's newsletter, sent to hundreds of teachers and departmental heads in New Zealand. The subsequent debate spilled over into the national news media, and even on to the website of Britain's Simplified Spelling Society, which has long campaigned against what it calls the public (**2**) of non-American spellings.

Paragraph E

The call for change comes at a time when local-language educators are (**5**) both an (**6**) of general interest in American language themes and a general decline in the overall popularity of English as a subject. According to figures released this year by the country's education ministry, the number of senior secondary school pupils studying English has fallen over the past decade from nearly 100% to about 92%. At university entrance level the number stands at 60%, down from 70% in 1990. At the post-secondary level the country's eight universities and 35 polytechnics are increasingly concerned about the literacy levels and communication skills of incoming students, according to Frances Kelly, a policy manager with the ministry.

The decline parallels New Zealand's overall literacy rate, which, as measured by international agencies, has decreased over the past 10 years from a perfect 100% to today's 98%.

Paragraph F

The suggestion has been made at the behest of the New Zealand Association of English Teachers, whose president, Phil Coogan, is impressed by the 'phonetic (**1**)' of American spelling and, thanks to the internet, its global ubiquity. The issue, he believes, 'is going to become increasingly important, especially with the widespread use of electronic language'.

Paragraph G

Coogan, who believes his association will indeed (**7**) one of the proposed changes later this year – a move that would then need to be endorsed by the country's governing qualifications authority – insists that standards of communication are not at issue, and that there will never be room among his colleagues for an anything-goes attitude to teaching English. 'A mistake in written English is still a mistake,' he says. 'This is not about lowering standards, nor is it about issues of national identity. It would be a shame if the subject gets clouded over in either of these ways.'

David Cohen

Source: *The Guardian Weekly*, June 2002

7   How did you decide on the order? What clues did you find in the text? Check the order with other people in your class.

8 Look at each gap in the text more carefully. What type of word or phrase is required to complete each one? Use the seven words from Exercise 5 to complete the gaps. Check your answers with your partner.

9 Find the words which you corrected in Exercise 3 in the text. Were your corrections right?

10 Find words or phrases in the text which have a similar meaning to the following:

   a things that are slightly different from the usual (paragraph A)

   b existing in many places (F)

   c requested, asked for (D)

   d spread into other places and situations (D)

   e introduce something secretly (C)

   f given formal approval or support (G)

C Speaking

11 In the text, who says that:

   a he is impressed with the 'phonetic logic' of American spelling?

   b chaos will naturally follow?

   Who do you agree with? Why? How important do you think correct spelling is? Discuss with your partner.

12 Everyone makes mistakes, even in their first language. With your partner, discuss and make a list of the types of written language mistakes that you make, either frequently or rarely. Rank each one so that number 1 on your list is your most frequent language mistake.

   Example: 1 spelling, 2 paragraphs, 3 word order, etc.

13 Compare your list of language mistakes with other people's in your class. Are there any mistakes which are common to everyone? Which type of mistake is the least common?

14 Think about the mistakes you make in spoken language. Are there any similarities with your list from Exercise 12? What can you do to avoid making these mistakes?

D Writing: formal letter

15 What should the layout of a formal letter look like? What should be included in the introduction and the conclusion? How should the body of the letter deal with the subject? Discuss with your partner and draw a rough plan for a formal letter.

16 How do you begin a formal letter in English? What can you write after 'Dear …'? Look back at Exercise 13 in Unit 3. Which endings would be suitable for a *formal* letter?

17 Which of the following phrases would be appropriate in a formal letter?

a   I would be grateful if you would send me …

b   Send me …

c   I want some information about …

d   I would appreciate it if …

e   Please tell me …

f   It would be useful if you could inform me …

g   How much does …?

h   Give me …

18 Look at this **exam-type question**. What exactly do you have to do? Discuss with your partner, but do *not* write anything yet.

Improve Your Spelling!

Do you want to improve your spelling?

Would you like to be able to throw away your dictionary and not worry any more about making spelling mistakes?

Would you like to help your friends and work colleagues with their spelling?

Yes?

Then write for more information about our courses today!

The English Spelling Society – ESS
578 Oxford Street, Birmingham BS3 8YG
info@ess.com

Write a letter to the ESS in which you:

• explain why you are interested in getting more information

• ask for more details about ESS courses (prices, length, materials, etc.)

Write about 150–200 words for the Extended curriculum and 100–150 words for the Core curriculum.

---

19 Look at the letter on page 68 written by a student in response to the question in Exercise 18. The writer of this letter has made some spelling and grammar mistakes. There are also some mistakes in the layout and the language used. With your partner, identify and correct the spelling and grammar mistakes. Do *not* rewrite the letter.

Dear ESS

January 29

I have seen your advertisement today in my local newspaper magazine and want to get more information from you about the cources you offer people who want to improve their speling. I would like to be able to throw away your dictionary and not worry any more about making speing mistakes. I would like to help your friends and work colleagues with their speling.

I am a student who I am studyng english in college and my speling is not very good so I want to improve and write better english. I need to write compositions in english and I do not have time to use a dictionary all the time at home and at school. Please will you send me some informations about your cources, the prizes and lenth and the materials you will send me and tell me when I can start a cource with ESS. I am look forward to hear from you a.s.a.p.

Best wishes

Bruno

(164 words)

20   Look at the content and layout of the letter. How can they be improved? How can the language be made more formal? Work with your partner but do *not* rewrite the letter.

21   Look at this model answer to the question in Exercise 18. In what ways is it an improvement on the letter in Exercise 19?
Discuss with your partner.

Dear Sir or Madam

I have just seen your advertisement in today's 'Daily Courier' newspaper and I would be grateful if you could send me further information and details about your courses for people who want to improve their spelling and their friends' spelling.

I am a 16-year-old student studying English, geography and history at a college in Botswana. I am currently in my first year at college. My teachers tell me that I need to improve my spelling to make my writing better. Also, I find that using a dictionary at home and at college takes up a lot of very valuable time, and often it is difficult to find the word that I want. Furthermore, as I sometimes study with my classmates, I would also be able to help them when they have problems with their spelling.

I think one of your courses might be of use to me, and I would therefore appreciate it if you could forward to me some information about your courses, including full details of your prices, the length of the courses, and the study materials available.

I look forward to hearing from you in the very near future.

Yours faithfully

M. Gaobakwe

(200 words)

22 Read the job advertisement below. Write a letter of application for the job in which you:

- describe yourself and your qualifications
- say why you think you are suitable
- say when you are available for an interview and when you would be free to start work

Write about 150–200 word for the Extended curriculum and 100–150 for the Core curriculum.

VACANCY

Are you aged 16–19 with a school-leaving certificate? Want to join a well-known international sports company? Would you like to influence sports fashion over the next three years? Here's your chance!

We are looking for young, enthusiastic people with a real interest in sport and the sports clothing industry to join our Head Office. Your role will be to decide which new fashion designs should be sold in *Winning Sports* shops all over the country.

Why not contact us today for more details?

Winning Sports, 246 Arena Lane, Cairo, Egypt

tel: 246 1234, email: enquiries@winningsports.com

Remember the rules for writing this type of letter:

- use formal language
- no slang
- no abbreviations
- use an appropriate beginning and ending
- You will not usually be required to write an addresses or date for this task in the exam

 E Speaking: job interview

23 You are going to act out a job interview with your partner. Read the instructions for Student A or Student B on page 70 – your teacher will tell you which role is yours. Then, join up with some other students who have the same role, and discuss the type of language you will use during the interview. Write down your ideas.

STUDENT A	STUDENT B
I've enjoyed studying X at school …	What are your interests?
I think fashion designs these days are …	Have you studied X at school?

24 When you are ready, join up with a student playing the other role, and act out the interview using the guidelines below:

Student A: Your letter of application for the job in Exercise 22 has been successful and you are going to have an interview. Your partner is going to interview you. Prepare yourself for the interview, paying particular attention to the points made in the job advertisement. Be prepared to give details of your exam qualifications, and to say why you want this particular job. Also, think about what experience you already have of sport: are you a player, or a spectator?

Student B: You are the Personnel Manager at *Winning Sports* and you are going to interview your partner for the job advertised. Prepare the questions for the interview, paying particular attention to the points made in the job advertisement. You will need to ask questions about your partner's exam qualifications, their experiences of sport, and their reasons for wanting this particular job.

F Further practice

25 Read the text 'Are you a poor talker?' and answer the questions which follow.

Are you a poor talker?

A simple technique for acquiring a swift mastery of everyday conversation and writing has been announced. It can pay you real dividends in both social and professional advancement. It works like magic to give you added poise, self-confidence and greater popularity. The details of this method are described in a fascinating book, *Adventures in Speaking and Writing*, sent free on request.

Many people do not realise how much they could influence others simply by what they say and how they say it. Those who realise this radiate enthusiasm, hold the attention of their listeners with bright, sparkling conversation that attracts friends and

opportunities wherever they go. Whether in business, at social functions, or even in casual conversation with new acquaintances, there are ways in which you can make a good impression every time you talk.

After all, conversation has certain fundamental rules and principles – just like any other art. The good talkers whom you admire know these rules and apply them whenever they converse. Learn the rules and you can make your conversation brighter, more entertaining and impressive. Then you could find yourself becoming more popular and winning new friendships in the business and social worlds.

To acquaint all readers of this newspaper with the easy-to-follow rules for developing skill in everyday conversation and writing, we, the publishers, have printed full details of this interesting self-training method in a fascinating book, *Adventures in Speaking and Writing*, sent free on request. No obligation. Just telephone 0800 298 7070 free, or fill in and return the coupon on page 13 (no stamp needed). Or write to: Effective Speaking Programme, Dept MGS10T, FREEPOST 246, London WC1A 1BR.

a In what situations can the new technique improve your conversation skills?

b Where can you get more details about the method for improving your speaking and writing skills?

c In what **two** ways does the text say that you can influence others?

d In what ways is conversation like any other art?

e Why have the publishers printed details of the training methods in a book?

f How can you obtain more information? Give **three** ways.

26 Using the text 'Are you a poor talker?' give another meaning for each of the following phrases. Use your dictionary for help. Then, use each one in a sentence of your own which makes its meaning clear.

   a   pay dividends   c   radiate enthusiasm

   b   work like magic   d   make a good impression

27 You have seen this advertisement about a new magazine for teenagers.

TEEN WEEKLY!

New magazine for teenagers all over the world!

Stories, Movie star biographies, Sports gossip, Competitions, Problem page, and Lots more!

We are looking for people who are interested in these topics to join our team of young writers.

If you think you can write for teenagers, contact us today for more details.

Teen Weekly, 912 Riddle Road, London SW16 4RT

vacancies@teenweekly.co.uk

Write a letter to *Teen Weekly* in which you:

• describe why you think you are suitable for the job

• request more details about the job

• ask for information about the application procedure

Write about 150–200 words for the Extended curriculum and 100–150 words for the Core curriculum.

28 Read the letter below, which was printed in a weekly newspaper. Write a letter to the Editor in response, expressing your own opinion of young people today and commenting on the views of the writer. Write about 150–200 words for the Extended curriculum and 100–150 words for the Core curriculum.

> Dear Sir
>
> I am writing to complain about the crowds of young hooligans who meet outside the 'Café New' in Market Street on a Friday night.
>
> Last Friday I was walking along Market Street at about 9pm when I noticed a crowd of perhaps ten or twelve of these young troublemakers, standing around talking to each other, smoking and chewing gum. As I approached they made no effort whatsoever to get out of my way, and I had to go off the pavement into the road to get past them!
>
> Not only is this sort of behaviour totally unacceptable, but it is also an indication of the laziness which we are seeing in young people today. When I was a teenager, we used our free time constructively, and we knew how to be polite to our elders and superiors. As for smoking and chewing gum, they were unheard of. These louts should find themselves a responsible job and learn some decent manners.
>
> Yours faithfully

Unit 9: *Focus on listening skills*

Exam Part 3
In this unit we will concentrate on listening skills and on the true/false questions you may have in Part 3 of the IGCSE Listening paper (Core option only). In Part 3 of the Listening paper, you may need to recognise and distinguish between facts, opinions and ideas.

A Speaking

1 The following newspaper cuttings are taken from the job advertisement pages. What do they all have in common? Discuss with your partner.

SENIOR WEB DESIGNER

Expanding London design agency requires fluent web designer to work on a range of accounts from the financial sector to on-line 'style' magazines. Must have strong communication skills and deliver on time/budget. Ability to integrate programming skills into print support media a big advantage, as the agency offers a range of 'integrated services'. You must be organised, self-motivated and fast with a strong track record.
We offer a small team, responsibility, prestigious clients and, best of all, an excellent salary package.

Skills list: PhotoShop, Quark, Illustrator, Dreamweaver, Flash, Html

e-mail CV to mac@pts.co.uk

A | CREATIVE | MAC | DESIGNER

is required by a small but ambitious design company specialising in travel and leisure. An enthusiasm for good design, attention to detail and the usual set of mac skills to implement your ideas are essential, with at least two years working experience. New media skills would be an advantage and system knowledge even better. Email your CV along with samples of your **best** work to:

nicky@workcreative.com

Or via pen and paper to:

Nicky Rea, WORK creative
Horspath Road, Oxford OX2 4QN

W O R K creative

Graphic Designer

with at least 3 years agency experience to create sizzling ads, great IDs, stunning posters and award winning literature. If you are keen, intelligent and talented with experience in Quark & P/Shop.

Salary in the region of £18k

Email CV now to:

steve@workline.net
or Fax: 09125 512263

Ronin Associates Ltd

1st floor, Unit 1–2 Colono Way, Watford, Herts

2 What is a CV? Check in your dictionary. Note: in some parts of the world a CV is known as a 'resumé'.

3 Discuss with your partner what information you think a CV should contain. Make a list of possible headings, for example 'Education'.

4 Compare your list with the headings given here. In what order do you think these headings should appear on a CV? You can check the order later.

- Education
- Hobbies
- Languages
- Work experience

- Personal information (name, date of birth, etc.)
- Qualifications
- Referees (people who will provide a reference for you)

Track 5

B Listening: radio interview

5 You are going to listen to a careers advisor at a school in Spain being interviewed on the radio. The first time you listen, check the order in which the CV areas from Exercise 4 appear.

6 Look at the true/false statements below. Read each one carefully and identify the key word/s in each statement. Do *not* write your answers yet.

   a Janine Mesumo only advises students on career options.

   b The important thing is to include as much detail as possible in a CV.

   c Many people forget to include their name on their CV.

   d Janine recommends listing education and qualifications together.

   e Students worry about not having any work experience.

   f It is not a good idea to mention weekend work.

   g Language skills should be included near the end of the CV.

7 Listen a second time. As you listen, decide if the statements above are true or false. Check your answers with your partner.

8 Read the transcript on pages 160–161 and check your answers.

C Writing: CV

9 You now know what information should go in a CV and the order in which it should appear. Discuss with your partner the information which you would put in your own CV. Think also about the details that you would *not* include!

10 Write your own CV. Include information in the following areas: personal details, education, qualifications, work experience, hobbies and interests, referees. Read your partner's CV. Has s/he included all the necessary information?

D Listening: job interview

Track 6

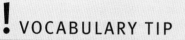

VOCABULARY TIP

Notice how the word 'interviewer' changes to 'interviewee'. When spoken, the stress on these two words is different:

interviewer   interviewee

Other examples are employer and employee.

There are a small number of these 'person' nouns in English which end in '-ee'. Can you think of any more?

11 You are going to listen to a student being interviewed for the job advertised in Unit 8 Exercise 22. Before you listen, decide with your partner and make notes about what questions the interviewer might ask the interviewee.

12 What information do you think the interviewee should give the interviewer? Before you listen, decide with your partner and make notes.

13 Listen to the interview. As you listen, make notes about the mistakes the interviewee makes during the interview.

14 Listen again, this time without the interviewee's responses to the interviewer's questions. What would you say in response to the questions? Look back at your notes in Exercise 12.

E Speaking: job interview

15   *Student A:* You are going to be interviewed by your partner for the job advertised in Unit 8 Exercise 27. Using the CV you have already written, answer the interviewer's questions.

Student B: You are going to interview your partner for the job advertised in Unit 8 Exercise 27. Use your partner's CV to ask questions.

Try to record or video the interview!

F Reading

16   Read the following article about CVs from different countries. Copy the table on page 75 and, as you read, complete the first two columns. Do *not* worry about the third and fourth columns at the moment.
An example has been done for you.

CVs from around the world

Did you know that your CV needs to be adapted depending on where in the world you are looking for a job? The Germans, French, Americans and Italians all look for different things, despite the fact that we are living in a global village. Small cultural differences still apply. And although Britain is part of Europe, it takes its business philosophy from America – the 'can do' approach which does not always go down well with other European countries.

Another problem for the British is their lack of skills in foreign languages, a fact which makes European employers have a rather low opinion of people applying from the UK. So, if you do have language skills, these should be highlighted in your CV, along with any foreign travel or cultural experiences. A CV should show that you are open to new cultures and ideas, so a summer job picking grapes in France, or a voluntary post helping sick children in another part of the world, should be highlighted.

Even within Europe, there are enormous differences in what is expected of applicants for jobs. In France, companies expect you to supply a handwritten cover letter, as they are very keen on obtaining information from the way in which people write. You will be expected to list personal interests, as well as any languages you speak, and provide them with a photograph.

The Germans, on the other hand, do not expect a cover letter. However, they do demand that your CV is presented in a binder, together with copies of all your education certificates and references from previous employers. German companies require information which in the UK would not be requested until a job offer was going to be made. German employers are not interested in your personal interests, but often applicants include details about their parents and their parents' jobs.

Italy and Spain are strong on personal contacts, so if you are planning to apply for a job in one of these countries it would be a good idea to go there and meet people. Italians accept that you might not know their language, but if you are willing to learn, they will accept that. In Italy trust is very important, as well as dressing well and having good manners. In Scandinavian cultures, especially Norway, your CV should not be self-centred, seeking to sell the individual with words like 'committed'. Norwegians expect you not to overplay your achievements.

In the USA, some of what British people include in their CVs would be illegal. Basically, anything which might give prospective employers a chance to discriminate against you should be excluded. This means you should exclude details such as age, sex or marital status, and never include a photograph. Any of these could give someone grounds for discrimination against you. The aim of an American CV (known as a 'resumé') is to show that you can do the job.

COUNTRY/CONTINENT	NATIONALITY	INCLUDE	EXCLUDE
Germany	German	references	cover letter

17 Read the text again and complete the information in your table (not all the spaces can be filled). Compare it with your partner's. Have you included similar information?

18 Work with your partner. Find words or phrases in the text which have a similar meaning to the following. Use your dictionary for help.

a   worldwide (paragraph 1)

b   understanding, knowledge (2)

c   without payment (2)

d   file, folder (4)

e   personal connections (5)

f   exaggerate the importance of something (5)

g   expected, likely (6)

h   treat unfairly (6)

 ## G Further practice

19 Which country's attitude to CV writing do you think is most sensible? Find out about CVs in your country – what should be included and excluded? Prepare a talk of two to three minutes on the subject of CV writing around the world.

20 Write a letter to your friend describing the interview you had in Exercise 15. Include information about the job, the type of questions the interviewer asked you, and how you replied. What was the outcome of the interview? Did you get the job? Write 150–200 words, (100–150 for the Core curriculum).

21 Think of a famous person whom you would like to know more about. Find out as much information as possible about the person, and then write their CV. Think about where you can obtain information. The internet? Your school library? Books and magazines at home?

22 Imagine that you have been given the chance to interview the famous person you chose in Exercise 21 for your school newsletter or magazine. Write a list of about ten questions which you would like to ask them.

Unit 10: *Exam practice*

In this unit you will have the opportunity to do some examination practice with exam-type questions. These will focus on the examination areas covered in the previous four units: exam exercises 2 (reading), 3 (reading and writing), 6 and 7 (writing) and listening (Part 2).

For information on how you will be assessed in the examination, see Unit 5.

Reading: Exam exercise 2 (Extended option)

1   The following article is about the way in which technology is changing. Read it carefully and then answer the questions which follow.

GOODBYE BARCODES, HELLO TRANSMITTERS

Razor blades and medicines packaged with pinpoint-sized computer chips and tiny antennae that may eventually send shopkeepers and manufacturers a wealth of information about the products (and people who buy them) have started appearing in shops and supermarkets.

Within two decades, the minuscule transmitters are expected to replace the familiar product barcodes, and retailers are already envisioning the conveniences that the new technology, called 'radio frequency identification' (RFID), will bring, even though some people are raising questions about personal privacy.

A shopworker will know immediately when the milk on the shelf has expired, for example, and can replace it before a customer picks it up. Shops could quickly remove damaged products, or ones which have expired,

especially important with products such as health-care items.

RFID technology builds upon the Uniform Product Code (UPC) symbol and barcodes that, when read by a scanner, enable manufacturers and retailers to keep up with their prices and inventory of products. A computer chip smaller than the head of an ant and a thin antenna attached to a bottle,

box, can or package will alert retailers and suppliers when a product is taken off a shelf or moved from a storeroom. A radio signal is beamed to an electronic receiver, which then delivers a message to a computer in the store or factory.

However, RFID technology is not new. The tiny chips and small antennae are already familiar to workers equipped with security cards that, when waved in front of a receiver, unlock the doors of their offices or send information to a security guard.

Homes equipped with receivers could alert us when we are running out of orange juice, or when an important medicine is about to expire. When the receivers are connected to a national network, it is feasible that products we are about to run out of at home could be delivered automatically. Furthermore, the at-home devices could supply details to marketers about a family's eating and hygiene habits.

The main concern is that of privacy. One way to address this would be to allow consumers to disable the computer chips once they leave the shop where they bought the product. Any technology can be abused, but most people feel that the benefits of RFID technology far outweigh any privacy concerns, for both the consumer and the retailer.

Source: Adapted from *The Cyprus Weekly*, 18–24 July 2003. Reprinted with permission of the Associated Press

a   When is it expected that barcodes on products will be replaced by the new technology? **[1]**

b   Despite the advantages of RFID, what worries some people about it? **[1]**

c   Give **three** examples of what the new technology will be able to do in shops. **[2]**

d   What **two** components does RFID technology use? **[1]**

e   What happens once the radio signal is sent to the electronic receiver? **[1]**

f   Give **two** ways in which RFID technology is already in use. **[2]**

g   In what **four** ways could home-based RFID technology change our lifestyles? **[2]**

h   Write a paragraph of about 60 words in which you outline **four** points about RFID technology. **[4]**

[Total: 14]

2   The following article is about the technology used to recycle tin cans. Read it carefully and then answer the questions which follow.

RECYCLING TINS

Tinplate is used for many different purposes. For instance, cans for fruit or vegetables, caps for bottles, screw caps for jars and the sides and bases of beverage cans are all manufactured from tinplate – a term that stands for tin-coated steel.

The steel is first rolled into thin sheets of metal that are between 0.5 and 1.5 millimetres in thickness. Each square metre of thin sheet is coated with 2 grams of tin to produce tinplate. After being shaped into containers and before being filled, the tin cans are painted or 'lacquered' on the inside to prevent corrosion and to rule out any changes in taste to the product.

When heat was first used to sterilise canned products, this led to a breakthrough in the industrial production of tin cans for the packaging of food. Canned food was launched on the market as long ago as 1830, and, for a long time, anything sold in a tin can was an expensive delicacy. The first tinplate drinks can was developed in 1935.

Ever since it was first produced, tinplate has been recycled because it can easily be melted down and then recycled as often as desired without any loss in quality. In Germany, the use of recycled tinplate saves about 6 million tonnes of coal per year. Between 15 and 17 million tonnes of steel are melted down and recycled each year.

Before tinplate packaging can be recycled, it needs to be sorted. The technique used is based on a well-known phenomenon – magnetism. Tinplate is an iron product, and is therefore magnetic. Overhead magnets are generally used to remove tin cans from the passing stream of lightweight packaging on a conveyor belt. These overhead magnets, which are positioned across the conveyor belt, attract and lift the tin cans.

The sorted cans are pressed into tinplate blocks weighing 200 kg and transported to factories, where the tinplate is used to produce steel. Huge magnets lift the 200 kg blocks or 'bales' of tinplate and place them in ovens (known as 'converters') which have been heated to 1,600° Celsius. The tinplate melts and is poured into an over-sized pan, and at the end of the process a glowing, burning brick or 'ingot' is discharged: 1.2 m wide, 25 cm thick and 23 tonnes in weight. The ingots are rolled into thin sheets. Up to

300,000 new tin cans for food products can be manufactured from each ingot.

Even a tried and tested recycling process can be improved on, however, and the recycling of tinplate packaging is continuously being developed and improved.

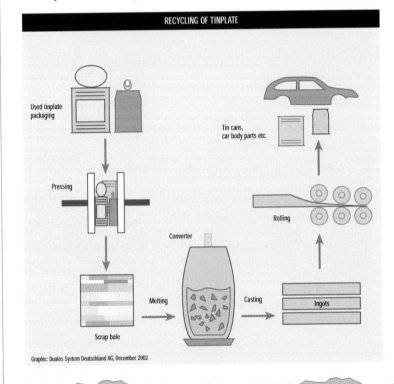

RECYCLING OF TINPLATE

Graphic: Duales System Deutschland AG, December 2002

RECYCLING OF TINPLATE IN GERMANY (tonnes)	
1995	259,100
1996	301,800
1997	312,100
1998	374,800
1999	322,314
2000	318,086
2001	314,347
2002	314,859

Source: Adapted from *Packaging Recycling*, December 2002

a Name **four** types of packaging that are made from tinplate. **[1]**

b What happens to steel in order to produce tinplate? Name **two** things. **[2]**

c Give **two** reasons why tin cans are lacquered on the inside. **[1]**

d Why has tinplate always been recycled? **[1]**

e How much coal is saved each year in Germany through the use of recycled tinplate? **[1]**

f Why is magnetism so important in the tinplate sorting and recycling process? **[2]**

g How much do the ingots weigh? **[1]**

h How much tinplate was recycled in Germany in 2000? **[1]**

i Make a list of **four** things that happen to the 200 kg blocks of tinplate during the recycling process. **[4]**

[Total: 14]

Reading and writing: Exam exercise 3 (Core and Extended)

Read the following information about Ahmed Hassan, who wants to apply for a job he has seen advertised in his local newspaper *The Gulf Daily Times*. He lives in Dubai, one of the United Arab Emirates, at 23 Al Falaj Street, and his mobile telephone number is 73-918247. Ahmed's email address is Ahmed@dubainet .com He was born on 19 October 1985, and has lived in Dubai all his life.

Ahmed left Dubai High School at the age of 16, after he had taken his IGCSE examinations in Arabic (First Language), Maths, History, Physics and French (Foreign Language). He achieved Grade D in all subjects, except for Arabic (Grade C). He also achieved a Grade C for IGCSE English as a Second Language. While he was at school he was president of the debating society, and organised a group called 'Let's Recycle!'

Ahmed is very interested in football, and he enjoys using the internet to find out more about his country and the Arabic language.

If his job application is successful, it will be his first employment and he wants to start as soon as possible.

Ahmed has seen the following job advertisement, and has obtained an application form.

Imagine you are Ahmed. Copy and complete the application form.

THE GULF DAILY TIMES, DUBAI

Required immediately
Trainee Journalist

to assist with research in our busy local news department

Apply to the Editor,
The Gulf Daily Times, PO Box 1310, Dubai

WRITE FOR AN APPLICATION FORM
BEFORE THE CLOSING DATE OF 31 JULY.

APPLICATION FORM
THE GULF DAILY TIMES, DUBAI

JOB APPLIED FOR:

PERSONAL DETAILS

NAME (BLOCK CAPITALS PLEASE):

ADDRESS:

MOBILE:

EMAIL:

DATE OF BIRTH:

EDUCATION

NAME OF SCHOOL:

QUALIFICATIONS:

POSITIONS OF RESPONSIBILITY AT SCHOOL:

HOBBIES AND INTERESTS:

IF YOU ARE OFFERED THE JOB, CAN YOU START WORK IMMEDIATELY? (PLEASE TICK)

YES ☐   NO ☐

Writing: Exam exercise 6 or 7

1   Write a letter to the Editor of *The Gulf Daily Times* to support your application for the job of Trainee Journalist (see previous question). In your letter give **three** reasons why you think you are suitable for the position. Write between 150 and 200 words. Do not include addresses.

2   You have heard that a new supermarket in your town is offering a course about healthy eating to all its customers. During the course, you will learn what healthy food is, and how to prepare healthy meals at home. You think it would be useful for you and your school classmates to attend the course.

Write a letter to the supermarket asking for more information. In your letter:

* ask when the course takes place and how much it costs

* ask who can join the course and if there are any age restrictions

* say why you think it would be useful for you and your friends to attend, and what you hope to learn from it

Your letter should be 150–200 words long for the Extended curriculum and 100–150 words for the Core curriculum.

Listening: Part 2

Track 7

Core questions

Listen to the interview on tigers in India, by Sanjit Roy, a tiger expert, and decide whether each statement is **true** or **false**. You will hear the interview twice.

a	The number of tigers in India is decreasing.	[1]
b	Tigers used to be killed for their fur.	[1]
c	Talcum powder is an important ingredient in make-up and toiletries.	[1]
d	Talcum powder does not come from tigers.	[1]
e	Marble and other stones are the source for talcum powder.	[1]
f	Tigers are threatened by talcum powder taken from marble.	[1]
g	It will take longer than ten years for the tiger to become extinct.	[1]
h	Dynamite is used in the tigers' habitat.	[1]
i	The tigers' natural habitat is protected by environmental laws.	[1]
j	An adult male needs more than 100 km^2 in which to hunt.	[1]
k	Nothing can be done to save the Indian tiger.	[1]
l	Some marble mines are being closed.	[1]

[Total: 12]

Extended questions

Listen to the interview on tigers in India, by Sanjit Roy, a tiger expert, and answer the questions which follow. You will hear the interview twice.

a   How many tigers are left in India?   [1]

b   Why were tigers hunted in the past?   [1]

c   Where does talcum powder come from?   [1]

d   When does Sanjit predict that the Indian tiger will become extinct?   [1]

e   What is dynamite used for?   [1]

f   What effect does the loss of habitat have on tigers?   [1]

g   Why can very little be done to save the Indian tiger?   [1]

[Total: 7]

Unit 11: *Focus on reading skills*

Exam Exercises 1 and 2
In this unit we will concentrate on the more detailed reading of texts.

A Speaking

1 The *Guinness Book of World Records* is famous all over the world. What is a 'record'? Do you know the details of any records? Discuss with your partner.

2 What record would you like to break? For example, would you like to be the tallest person in the world? Or the person who can speak the most languages? Or the person to score the most goals in a match? Or the person who can eat the most doughnuts without licking their lips?! Discuss with your partner and be prepared to give feedback to the group.

3 Quiz! With your partner, choose the answer which you think best completes the following statements about world records and record breaking.

a The longest ever spacewalk lasted:

   45 minutes   2 hours 21 minutes   8 hours 29 minutes

b The Atlantic squid's eyes have a diameter of:

   25 cm   50 cm   75 cm

c The largest yo-yo ever made weighs:

   251 kg   407 kg   639 kg

d A man in the USA stayed on a tightrope for:

   105 days   205 days   305 days

e …… million people died of influenza worldwide between 1918 and 1919.

   21.64   32.89   48.62

4 Quickly skim these short texts to check your answers to the quiz in Exercise 3.

A 407-kg (896-lb) yo-yo with a diameter of 3.17 m (10 ft 5 in) was devised by JN Nichols (Vimto) Ltd and made by students at Stockport College, Greater Manchester, UK. It was launched by crane from a height of 57.5 m (189 ft).

The Atlantic giant squid (*Architeuthis dux*) has larger eyes than any other animal. A record-breaking specimen found in Thimble Tickle Bay, Newfoundland, Canada, in 1878, had eyes with an estimated diameter of 50 cm (20 in).

The longest spacewalk ever undertaken was one of 8 hr 29 min, by Pierre Thuot, Rick Hieb and Tom Akers of STS 49 Endeavor, on May 13, 1992. The longest Soviet attempt lasted 7 hr 16 min in 1990.

Between 1918 and 1919, 21.64 million people died worldwide of influenza.

Source: *Guinness Book of World Records*

The world tightrope endurance record is 205 days, set by Jorge Ojeda-Guzman of Orlando, Florida, USA. He walked on an 11-m (36-ft) long wire, which was 10.7 m (35 ft) above the ground.

B Reading

5   You are going to read about a man called Rod Baber who has climbed to the top of the highest mountain in every European country. The following words and phrases appear in the text. With your partner, discuss what these words mean. Use your dictionary as well.

a   volatile regions

b   treacherous

c   altitude sickness

d   conquered

e   potential sponsors

f   venture

g   summit

h   sheer determination

6   True or false? Before you read, decide with your partner if the following statements are likely to be true or false. Do they seem reasonable to you? Why/Why not? Be prepared to give reasons for your decisions. There are some clues to help you.

a   Baber climbed 47 European mountains. (How many countries are there in Europe?)

b   It took him three years to achieve the world record. (How long would it take to climb so many mountains?)

c   He started his attempt in 1997.

d   He climbed 44 mountains in five months. (Would that be possible?)

e   The tallest mountain he climbed was 5,642 m. (Do you know how high the tallest mountain in Europe is?)

f   The top of Mt Ararat in Turkey is nearly 5 km above sea level.

g   Baber wants to climb the highest mountain in every country in the world. (What do you think? Does that surprise you?)

7   Scan the text 'The man who conquered every peak in Europe' and check your answers to Exercise 6.

The man who conquered every peak in Europe

During a daring two-month climbing expedition in some of Europe's most volatile regions, Rod Baber, a 29-year-old former telecom salesman, has survived rock falls and avalanches, sidestepped landmines and climbed one peak at night to avoid armed mountain patrols. He has spent a night on a treacherous one-metre ice ledge, battled altitude sickness and used Cuban cigars to bribe the shadowy figures who control mountain access.

For his troubles, he will enter the *Guinness Book of World Records* as the climber who has conquered the highest peak in each of the 47 European countries in the least time, shaving four years off the record of seven years that had been set two years previously.

It seems an extreme way to earn a place in the history books. The idea of doing the record started back in 1997, when Baber, who became a climbing fanatic in his teens after being sent on an adventure weekend, was spending an evening with some work colleagues. The conversation got around to climbing mountains and, from then on, he was hooked, and spent hours on the telephone to potential sponsors, trying to get them to agree to give him financial support for his venture.

Once he had received the first promise of money, Baber went into serious training. A panel of professional climbers was called in to draw up a list of the 47 peaks, which included Mt Elberus in Russia (5,642 m), the tallest mountain in Europe, and the highest point in Monaco, just 162 m, both of which he climbed along with 44 others during five months in 1998.

Frustratingly, weather and politics slowed him down. There were three left to do: 2,656 m Mt Daravica in Kosovo, whose slopes were studded with mines; Mt Shkhara in Georgia, whose steep sides make the 5,068 m ascent difficult and dangerous; and Mt Ararat in Turkey, whose summit is nearly 5 km above sea level.

Through a combination of support from local people, bribing officials, luck and sheer determination to achieve the record, Baber has done it. He does not see anything pointless or strange about his record. 'Work isn't challenging enough, and we all love a challenge. The most important thing is happiness, and I just love climbing,' says Baber, whose efforts raised several thousand pounds for various charities. He plans next to conquer the highest peak in every country in the world. He reckons he will be able to complete the remaining 199 peaks at the rate of a continent a year. 'I'd like to lead a normal life,' he says, 'but I'm on the mountain wagon now.'

Source: *Cyprus Review*, 1 September 2000

8   Scan the text again and find the words and phrases from Exercise 5. Do the meanings you discussed with your partner make sense in context?

9   Answer the following questions. Remember that you should keep your answers short, but you must include all the necessary information. Find the key word/s in each question before you begin.

   a   What was Baber's job before he began his record attempt?

   b   Name **three** problems that Baber faced during his attempt.

   c   Why is Baber in the *Guinness Book of World Records*?

   d   What started Baber's interest in mountaineering?

   e   Why did Baber spend hours on the telephone?

   f   Who decided which mountains Baber should climb?

g What problem did Baber face when he climbed Mt Daravica?

h What was particularly difficult about climbing Mt Shkhara?

i Apart from luck, what else helped Baber achieve his goal? Name **two** things.

j Who benefited from Baber's achievement?

C Reading and vocabulary

10 Robert Scott (1868–1912) made a successful attempt to reach the South Pole, only to find that another explorer (Roald Amundsen) had got there one month before him. Unfortunately, Scott and his team of explorers all perished on their return journey. You are going to read about this tragic event. Before you read, match the following words, which appear in the text, with the definitions. There are two extra definitions which you do *not* need to use.

a	stumbled	i	the action of cutting off a person's arm or leg
b	blizzard	ii	written clearly enough to be read
c	dissuade	iii	severe snow storm
d	amputation	iv	full of liquid or gas
e	rations	v	a place where food and other things are stored
f	depot	vi	try to stop someone from doing something
g	legible	vii	a situation where something cannot continue
		viii	walked unsteadily and almost fell
		ix	a fixed amount of food or water

Robert Scott: the return journey

Things got worse as the north wind continued to blow in their faces. Wilson was now becoming weak so Scott and Bowers had to make camp by themselves. The temperature fell to –43°F. On March 16 or 17 (they lost track of the days) Oates said he couldn't go on and wanted to be left in his bag. The others refused and he struggled on. There was a blizzard blowing in the morning when Oates said, 'I am just going outside and may be some time,' and he stumbled out of the tent. Scott wrote, 'We knew that poor Oates was walking to his death, but though we tried to dissuade him, we knew it was the act of a brave man.' Oates was never to be seen again.

On March 20 they awoke to a raging blizzard. Scott's right foot became a problem and he knew that 'these are the steps of my downfall'. Amputation was a certainty, 'but will the trouble spread? That is the serious question.' They were only 11 miles from a food camp but the blizzard stopped them from continuing on. They were out of oil and only had two days' rations. 'Have decided it shall be natural – we shall march for the depot and die in our tracks,' wrote Scott. They did not march again and on March 29 Scott made his last entry: 'It seems a pity, but I do not think that I can write more. R. Scott. For God's sake look after our people.' On another page he scribbled, 'Send this diary to my widow.'

It was not until November 12 that the search party found Scott's tent all but buried in snow. When the tent was opened, the searchers saw three men in their sleeping bags. On the left was Wilson, his hands crossed on his chest; on the right, Bowers, wrapped in his bag. It appeared that both had died peacefully in their sleep. But Scott was lying half out of his bag with one arm stretched out – he had been the last to die.

Remarkably, Scott had been able to find the strength, despite being half-starved and three-quarters frozen, to write 12 complete, legible letters. In one of these he wrote: 'I may not have proved a great explorer but we have done the greatest march ever made and come very near to great success.'

11 Skim the text. Find the words from Exercise 10 and then note five more words which you find difficult. Discuss these words with your partner and use your dictionary to help you understand what they mean.

12 Skim the text again and answer the following questions:

   a How many explorers are mentioned?

   b Which explorer survived the longest?

13 Scan the text, then copy and complete the table below.

DATE	WHAT HAPPENED?
March 16 or 17	

14 Scan the text again and write short answers to the following questions. Remember your answers should be short, but must include all the necessary information. Find the key word/s in each question first.

   a Why did Scott and Bowers have to make camp by themselves?

   b Why are two dates given for the day when Oates began to struggle?

   c What was the weather like when Oates left the tent?

   d Why was Scott worried about his right foot?

   e What prevented Scott and his team from reaching the food camp?

   f What did Scott mean when he wrote 'Have decided it shall be natural'?

   g What did Scott want to happen to his written notes?

   h In what condition was the tent when the search team found it?

   i How many months after the death of the team were their bodies found?

   j Why was it remarkable that Scott wrote 12 letters?

 D Speaking

15 What do you think about Baber's and Scott's achievements? Would you describe them as heroes? Why/Why not?

16 Do you agree with the following definition of a hero/heroine?

   Someone admired for their bravery or abilities, particularly someone who has acted with great courage under difficult or dangerous conditions.

   Do you think that Baber and Scott fit this definition?

17 What qualities do you think make someone a hero/heroine? Do they have to be brave? Could a coward be a hero? Are some heroes/heroines stupid or irresponsible?

18 Do you know (or know of) anyone whom you regard as a hero? What did s/he do? Why? What was the outcome? Does the person fit the definition in Exercise 16?

19 Read the following two paragraphs written by students. The first one thinks that Scott was a hero; the second one does not. What do you think?

Scott was a hero because of the incredible difficulties that he faced. During his attempt to return home after reaching the South Pole, he and his team had very little food and no oil for burning. The weather was extremely cold and Scott was forced to stay in his tent even though it was only 11 miles to base camp. Eventually Scott and his team all died in the tent, unable to move outside. They all showed great courage, strength and bravery.

Scott was not a hero because what he did was a hobby for him. I think a hero is someone who shows special qualities when doing something which is not a leisure activity. I believe what Scott did was hard work, and it was certainly dangerous, but he did it because he wanted to. There was no pressure on him and his team to suffer in the way that they did. They did not need to die in such a terrible way, nor put other people's lives in danger.

 E Writing

20 Choose a famous person whom you consider to be a hero/heroine. Then write a paragraph of no more than 100 words in which you give your reasons why you think this person is a hero/heroine.

21 Imagine you are Rod Baber. Write your diary entries for the days you climbed Mt Daravica and Mt Shkhara. Do not write more than about 100 words.

 F Further practice

22 Write a short piece describing the feelings of Scott's widow when she received the diary. Use details from the text. Do not write more than about 100 words.

23 What do you think about people participating in 'extreme sports' (sports which put people in some sort of danger)? Do people have the right to do this (as Scott did) in pursuit of their own goals? Be prepared to give your opinion to your group.

24 What do you think happened when Rod Baber had to bribe the mountain police? Write a dialogue between Baber and the 'shadowy figures who control mountain access'.

25 Read the following text about the first woman cosmonaut in space, the Russian Valentina Tereshkova. ('Cosmonaut' is another word for 'astronaut'.) Then decide if the statements which follow are true or false.

Valentina Tereshkova was born on 6 March 1937 in Maslennikovo, a small town in the Yaroslavl region of the former USSR. Her father, a tractor driver, was killed in action during World War II. Her mother, Elena Fedorovna, worked in a textile factory.

Valentina began school in 1945 in Yaroslavl at the age of eight. In 1953 she left school and began working, but continued her education by following a correspondence course. By 1961, she had gained a certificate in textile technology.

From an early age, Valentina was interested in parachute jumping and it was this interest that led to her career as a cosmonaut. She made her first parachute jump under the guidance of the local Aviation Club in Yaroslavl at the age of 22, on 21 May 1959. Soon after, she set up the Textile Mill Workers' Parachute Club and became its first committee leader. She was one of five women selected as cosmonaut-candidates on 16 February 1962. All five underwent the complete course of training, including weightless flights, parachute jumps, isolation tests, and centrifuge tests. While Valentina excelled in the physical training, she had more difficulty with rocket theory and spacecraft engineering. The training included 120 parachute jumps and pilot training with jet fighters.

On 14 June 1963, the rocket *Vostok 5* was launched with cosmonaut Valeri Bykovsky aboard, and two days later, Valentina Tereshkova became the first woman in space aboard *Vostok 6*. The Russian space federation was unhappy with Tereshkova's performance and she was not permitted to take manual control of the spacecraft as had been planned. However, she completed three days in space, more than the flight time of all the American astronauts put together.

It had been planned for *Vostok 5* to stay a record eight days in space, but Bykovsky had trouble with his heat regulation system and had to return to Earth after five days, only three hours after *Vostok 6*.

Tereshkova married Andrian Nikolayev, the only bachelor cosmonaut to have flown in space, on 3 November 1963, and on 8 June 1964 Valentina gave birth to a daughter, Elena Andrianovna, who later went on to become a doctor. But the marriage did not last long and the 'space family' fell apart.

Valentina obtained a college-level education at the Zhukovskiy Military Air Academy from 1964 to 1969, and after her graduation, in October 1969, the female cosmonaut crew was disbanded. Although an all-female flight was considered aboard a Voskhod spacecraft in 1965, this was cancelled after the near-disastrous flight of *Voskhod 2*.

a Valentina's education finished in 1953.

b Her first job was as a parachute jumper.

c She began her training as a cosmonaut in 1962.

d Valentina had some problems with parts of the cosmonaut training course.

e Valentina's first space flight was in *Vostok 5*.

f Valentina was supposed to take manual control of the spacecraft.

g *Vostok 5* stayed in space longer than *Vostok 6*.

h Valentina went into space again in 1969.

i *Voskhod 2* took a female crew into space in 1965.

Unit 12: *Focus on reading and writing skills*

Exam Exercises 4 and 5

 Ⓐ Reading

1   What qualities or characteristics do you think an entertainer or sportsperson needs to have? For example, do you think ambition is important? What about family and educational backgrounds? Money? Does an actor need to be good-looking? Discuss with your partner and make a list.

2   Look at this list of words taken from a text you are going to read about a sportsperson. Discuss the meaning of the words with your partner and use your dictionary for help.

impressive   trainee   influential   widespread   subsequent

3   Read the text below and complete the five numbered gaps with the words from Exercise 2.

David Robert Joseph Beckham was born in Leytonstone, England, on 2nd May 1975, and in 1989 he joined Manchester United's schoolboy squad. Two years later he became a (**1**) member of the full squad, and in January 1993, he became a professional footballer with one of the most famous football clubs in the world.

In the summer of 2002, Beckham led England out in the World Cup Finals in Japan and South Korea, not only as his country's captain, but as their most (**2**) player, as well as being possibly the most popular player in the UK. This was in complete contrast to his position after the 1998 World Cup in France, when he was sent off during the match against Argentina, and was held responsible by most supporters for England's (**3**) dismissal from the competition.

Source: *The Complete Encyclopedia of Manchester United Football Club,* 2002.

However, his ability to rise above the (**4**) abuse said much for his character and attitude, as he won over public opinion with a series of highly (**5**) displays in international matches.

---

4   Here is another text about a different type of entertainer. Look at this list of
    words and phrases taken from the text and try to decide what type of
    entertainer you are going to read about.

album   mesmerised audiences

child prodigy   music charts

classical, pop and jazz   orchestras

dramatic entry   repertoire

dressed unconventionally   TV appearances

exceptional achievement

5   The paragraphs of the text have been mixed up. Scan the text and put the
    paragraphs into a logical order. Do *not* worry about the gaps at the moment.

A

Vanessa has indeed come a long way to be what she is today. To date, she has released a
number of both classical and pop music albums. Her most recent release is a *Best of
Vanessa-Mae* collection, which includes the never released song *Art of War* and, as a
bonus, a video montage set to *Art of War*. Vanessa now also lists singing in her ……. ,
having added her voice to a number of tracks on her 2001 *Subject to Change* album.

B

Vanessa-Mae took the world by storm when she was just 16 with the release of her first
popular music album *The Violin Player*. Seen as a ……, many in the classical music
community were excited by this new star who had already released three classical CDs by
the time she was 13, had toured with orchestras and had made many TV appearances with
total professionalism.

C

Vanessa was 14 when she started working on *The Violin Player*. The album quickly reached
the top of the popular music charts in over twenty countries shortly after its release. In 1996,
she was nominated for the 'Best Female Artist' in the BRIT Awards. This was an …… as
Vanessa is the first classical musician to be nominated for this popular music award.

D

As Vanessa has progressed from child prodigy to independent adulthood, both she and her
music have matured. The personal strength and dynamic presence of Vanessa-Mae are
clear indicators of a musician who has fully arrived and is here to stay.

E

It was early in 1995 when Vanessa made her dramatic entry to the music scene with her
hugely popular and successful album *The Violin Player*. Classical music experts were appalled
that their child prodigy had released a popular music CD packaged as classical music. But the
world soon fell in love with Vanessa and her brand of music, a beautiful blend of ……
Vanessa …… with her compositions and charismatic personality. Vanessa also ……, causing
uproar from some music critics. But it is her mastery of the violin which continues to hold
listeners in awe.

F

Born on 27 October 1978 to a Thai father and a Chinese mother, Vanessa spent the first
three years of her childhood in Singapore, where she was born. At the age of three,
Vanessa moved with her mother to London, where she still resides.

6   Read the text again and complete the gaps with some of the words and phrases from Exercise 4. (You do not need to use all of them.) Check your answers with your partner.

7   Write answers to the following questions. Find the key word/s first. Remember to keep your answers short, but include all the necessary information. Check your answers with your partner.

   a   What is *The Violin Player*?

   b   What **three** things did Vanessa-Mae do before the release of *The Violin Player*?

   c   Why was her nomination as 'Best Female Artist' an exceptional achievement?

   d   Why were some classical music lovers upset by *The Violin Player*?

   e   Give **three** things which listeners particularly appreciate about Vanessa-Mae.

 B Writing: making notes

8   Look at this **exam-type question**. What exactly do you have to do? Do *not* write anything yet.

> Read the article and then write notes on the important events in Vanessa-Mae's life.

9   You are going to make some notes about Vanessa-Mae's life. First, discuss with your partner which of the following would be the *best* note for 27 October 1978. Be prepared to say why.

   a   Vanessa-Mae was born on 27 October 1978.

   b   born on 27 October 1978

   c   born

   d   born 27 October 1978

   e   Vanessa-Mae born

10   Now write notes about Vanessa-Mae's life. Put the events into chronological (time) order.

YEAR/AGE	EVENT

11   Compare your notes with your partner's. Have you included the same information? Check that you and your partner have written notes, and *not* full sentences.

C Speaking and vocabulary

12 What do the following words have in common? Discuss with your partner and add any similar words you can think of. Use your dictionary for help.

double   duo   identical

13 Did you add the word 'twin' to your list? What are twins? What term is used for three children born to the same mother at about the same time? What about four children? Five?

14 Do you know any twins or triplets? Have you noticed anything about their behaviour? Do they tend to behave in similar ways and have similar likes and dislikes?

15 It is sometimes said that one twin is 'good' while the other is 'bad'. This is obviously a myth, but twins are sometimes labelled in this way. You are going to read an article about the 'twin myth'. Before you do so, discuss the meaning of these words and phrases from the text with your partner. Use your dictionary for help.

a packaged as a pair

b polar opposites

c single-born

d public scrutiny

e individual potentials

f personality traits

g multiples

16 Match the words taken from the text (in the first column) with one of the definitions (in the second column). Discuss your choices with your partner.

a encounter	i let down
b compassion	ii meeting
c intrusive	iii unsuitable
d impulse	iv desire
e disenchanted	v interfering
f inappropriate	vi kindness

❶ Reading

17 Skim the text and find the words from Exercises 15 and 16. Do the meanings you agreed on with your partner fit the text? Do *not* worry about the words in brackets at the moment.

Good twin, bad twin

My first encounter with the myth that twins come packaged as a pair – one good and one bad – came more than 20 years ago in my local supermarket. As I pushed my shopping trolley with my 10-month-old twin daughters towards a woman, she said, 'Which one's the good one and which one's the bad one?' I was speechless and hurried past.

Twins are up against the human (enthuse) for comparing, contrasting and labelling people. Since twins are born a 'matched set', they are often seen as symbols of the good and bad in all of us. Ancient myths and modern movies are full of (situate) where twins are made to represent polar opposites.

Unfortunately, most people have more (familiarise) with twin myths than with living, breathing twins, who are, after all, just two little kids. As one mother of adult twin sons puts it, 'I was amazed at how good both my twins were. From an early age there was so much (care) and compassion between them.

If I offered one a biscuit, he wouldn't take it until he made sure that his brother was going to get one too. I tried, but I could never get my single-born kids to be as (think) of each other.' She says she protected her boys from intrusive public scrutiny and twin myths while they were growing up by giving them distinctly (differ) names. She never dressed them alike and avoided (emphasise) on their twinship.

Parents have the job of ensuring that their (multiply) have a chance to fulfil themselves, and to grow up to develop their individual potentials. To do that, parents need to get rid of any myths in the back of their minds, and to resist any impulse to favour one over the other. The key is to encourage each child to develop their strengths and (able), whether or not they are the same as the other twin's.

While few parents believe the myth of good twin/bad twin, some fall into the trap of contrasting their twins' personality traits and abilities: easy and difficult,

pretty and smart. Of course, there are times when any parent becomes disenchanted with one over the other. Wise parents keep these (feel) to themselves. When they speak of differences between their twin children, they translate them into positive points, and avoid negative labels. However, bad behaviour should always be disapproved of, as long as it is the behaviour, and not the child, which is the focus of the (disapprove).

Within the family, parents can control the (behave) of relatives who may believe in the twin myth. But there is no easy way to protect multiples from inappropriate questions and comments which they may meet outside the family circle. The best (defend) is to demonstrate a positive attitude towards twinship and about any differences between children. Perhaps you may never experience the twin myth, but if you do, be ready with a positive mind.

Source: Adapted from http://www.twinsmagazine.com/sample2.shtml, 18 September 2000

18 Look at the words in brackets in the text on page 93. All the words are verbs, but each one needs to be changed to a different part of speech in order to make sense in the text. Make a table as shown below. In it, write the correct form of each word, and say which part of speech it is. The first one has been done for you as an example. When you have completed the table, check your answers with your partner. Use your dictionary for help.

VERB	NEW WORD	PART OF SPEECH
enthuse	enthusiasm	noun
situate		
familiarise		
care		
think		
differ		
emphasise		
multiply		
able		
feel		
disapprove		
behave		
defend		

19 Answer the following questions. Keep your answers short but include all the necessary information. Remember to find the key word/s first.

a When did the writer first meet the twin myth?

b What made the writer speechless?

c Why are twins often symbolised as good and bad?

d What difference did the mother of adult twin sons notice between the twins and her other children?

e What trap do some parents fall into?

f What do wise parents do?

g What advice does the writer give about bad behaviour?

h In which situations is it not easy to protect twins from the twin myth?

i What is the best defence against the twin myth?

E Writing: summary

20 Look at this **exam-type question**. What exactly do you have to do? Do *not* write anything yet.

> Read the article and then write a summary of the advice given to parents about avoiding the twin myth.

21 Scan the text on page 93 and find the advice. You should be able to find at least eight pieces of advice. Discuss what you have found with your partner. Do you agree with each other?

22 Write your summary of the advice given to parents about the twin myth. Try to use your own words as far as possible, and do not write more than about 100 words.

F Speaking

23 What do you think about treating twins in the same way? Is it better to treat them differently? Why/Why not?

24 How far do you think that everyone in a family should be treated alike? What problems might arise? Should boys and girls expect to be treated differently?

25 What might be some of the advantages and disadvantage of being a twin? Would you like to be a twin or a triplet?

G Further practice

26 Look closely at the two pictures. Make notes about the **ten** ways in which A differs from B.

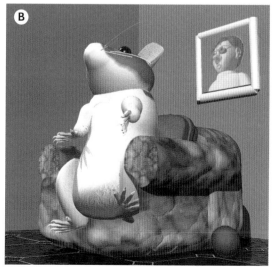

27 Write a detailed physical description of someone you know. It could be a family member or a friend. Write about 150–200 words for the Extended curriculum and 100–150 words for the Core curriculum.

28 Read the film summaries below. Use your dictionary to help you with any unknown words. Write three or four similar paragraphs describing cinema or TV films you have seen – but don't give away the endings!

'The Boys' Club'

Three teenagers hungry for excitement find all the thrills they need when a wounded fugitive hides in their den. When they find out he lied about being a cop on the run from criminals, they get an adventure they can do without.

'Good Will Hunting'

Will Hunting is a university janitor. When his genius for maths is discovered, a professor tries to help him change his life for the better, but does he want to be helped?

'My Ghost Dog'

Eight-year-old Toby's nasty aunt wants to take him away from his father so she can get her hands on his inheritance. When she hires thugs to kill his dog, Toby feels all alone, but Lucky comes back as a ghost to help him thwart his aunt's plans.

'Masterminds'

When terrorists seize an exclusive private school, their plans to hold the children hostage to their rich parents are threatened by a whizkid with a talent for computer hacking.

29 Read the text about Tom Cruise on page 97 and then answer the following questions. Find the key word/s first, and remember to keep your answers short but include all the necessary information.

a Why did Tom Cruise not stay in one place as a boy?

b What reason is given for Tom Cruise being introverted?

c Why was Cruise not able to follow a sports career?

d At what age would he have given up his acting career if he had not been successful?

e What reasons were given for refusing to offer Cruise any acting roles?

f What was Cruise's role in *Top Gun?*

g During which period did Cruise fail to convince critics of his acting ability?

h What made critics change their opinion of Cruise?

TOM CRUISE

Like a lot of film stars, it was Tom Cruise's bad start in life which gave him the ambition he needed to make it to the top. Born on 3 July 1962, Cruise was the only son of poor parents who moved around the US while his father looked for work. By the time Cruise was 14, he had been to 15 different schools in America. Unable to stay in one place long enough to make friends, Cruise became introverted and his life became even more miserable when he was diagnosed as suffering from a form of dyslexia.

When Cruise's mother and his stepfather moved to Glen Ridge, New Jersey, in 1977, the family settled for a while. Although not highly academic, Cruise excelled at sports, but a knee injury put paid to any hopes of a career in that field. He tried acting at school, and after appearing in a few plays, he thought he would try acting as a career. So, at the age of 18, he set himself a ten-year limit to make it in the acting world, and moved to New York.

At first he was turned down for role after role, dismissed for being too short, not handsome enough, or too serious. However, in 1981, he finally made his film debut in the Brooke Shields disaster *Endless Love*, and then went on to play small parts in other films. Five years later, his position as a film star was secured with *Top Gun*, where he played an elite military pilot, and *The Color of Money*, where he played alongside screen legend Paul Newman.

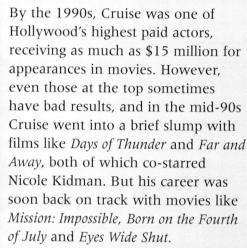

By the 1990s, Cruise was one of Hollywood's highest paid actors, receiving as much as $15 million for appearances in movies. However, even those at the top sometimes have bad results, and in the mid-90s Cruise went into a brief slump with films like *Days of Thunder* and *Far and Away*, both of which co-starred Nicole Kidman. But his career was soon back on track with movies like *Mission: Impossible, Born on the Fourth of July* and *Eyes Wide Shut*.

Now in his 40s, Cruise is one of the best-liked members of the Hollywood community. His role in *Mission: Impossible 2*, released in 2000, and its success, made it clear that the start of the new millennium was the start of a new era in Cruise's career. Critics who slammed his acting in earlier movies have agreed that he is now a major force in the acting profession.

Unit 13: *Focus on writing skills*

Exam Exercises 6 and 7

 A Speaking

1 Which international youth organisation do you think the following facts and figures relate to? The pictures above may help you if you are unsure.

   a First groups formed in 1908.

   b Over 100,000 members in the UK by 1910.

   c In the USA, 1 million members by 1930.

   d Originally for boys aged 11–18.

   e Other groups for girls and for younger boys set up in 1910 and 1914.

   f Founder of the movement died in 1941.

   g Nowadays, 10% of groups are mixed girls and boys.

   h Globally, membership is now over 34 million (including 9 million girls).

   i Groups exist in all but five countries of the world.

2 WOSM is the World Organisation of Scout Movements. WAGGGS is the World Association of Girl Guides and Girl Scouts. What do you know about them? Are you or any of your family or friends a member? With your partner and with other people in your group, discuss what WOSM and WAGGGS do. Make notes and be prepared to report back to your class.

 B Writing: paragraphs

3 Using only information from Exercise 1, write a short paragraph of not more than 100 words in which you explain the history of the WOSM and WAGGGS. Then write a second paragraph in which you include the information you collected from your group.

C Reading

4   The Guides and Scouts movements are global and have an enormous membership. Throughout the world they are involved in various assistance and money-raising projects. One of these is in the Asia-Pacific Region. Scan the text below in order to find out what the following figures refer to:

a   21 million km²   d   68%

b   1.9 billion   e   US$1 million

c   19 million   f   2005

Asia-Pacific Scouting Region: Regional Scout Foundation

Aim

To continually build capital funds through membership recruitment of individuals, national Scout organisations and their branches, and corporations who support the worthy cause of Scouting with their donations.

Objectives

a   To assist in funding worthwhile projects of Member Scout Organisations in the Asia-Pacific Region.

b   To support research projects on Scouting and the development of Scouting publications.

The creation

With a total area of more than 21 million km² and a population reaching 1.9 billion excluding non-member countries, the Asia-Pacific Scouting Region has the potential for a wide range of financial resources to support its undertakings. Having a total Scout membership of over 19 million, the region is responsible for 68% of the world's total Scouts. A vast population of young people is still to be reached. The Foundation started with an initial donation of US$10,000 in 1991, and in the following eight years raised a further US$1 million.

Goal

Having achieved the initial goal of US$1 million, the Regional Scout Committee has set itself the goal of raising a further US$1 million by 2005.

Management of the Foundation

A Management Committee oversees the affairs of the Foundation. The Scout Association of Hong Kong serves as the trustee while the World Scout Bureau (Asia-Pacific Regional Scout Office) is the secretariat.

Projects supported

The Regional Scout Foundation has supported an environment-oriented project in Bangladesh and a series of emergency training courses in the Philippines.

Foundation membership

The membership is open to individuals, national Scout organisations and their branches, and corporations.

For more information

Contact the Regional Scout Foundation at:

Regional Scout Foundation, Asia-Pacific Bureau, PO Box 4050, MCPO 1280, Makati City, Philippines, tel: (632) 818 0984/817 1675, fax: (632) 819 0093, e-mail: wsb@apr.scout.org

Source: Adapted from http://www.apr.scout.org.jp/foundation, 24 September 2000

5   Find words or phrases in the text which match the definitions below. Check your answers with your partner. Use your dictionary for help.

a   the finding of new people to work in or to join an organisation

b   smaller parts of an organisation

c   deserving of respect, admiration

d   usually money given in order to help

e the possibility for development

f promises to do something

g checks that work is done properly

h has control of property or money in an organisation

6 Read the following questions carefully and identify the key word/s in each one. Remember that there may be more than one key word in each question, and that the word or words from the text may have been rephrased. Then, find the key word/s in the text. Do *not* write anything yet.

a How does the Regional Scout Foundation aim to attract money?

b What are the RSF's **two** objectives?

c Why does the Asia-Pacific Scouting Region have so much potential for raising funds?

d What does the Regional Scout Committee hope to have done by 2005?

e In which **two** countries has the RSF given financial support to projects?

f Who can become a member of the RSF?

g How can you obtain more information about the RSF?

7 Check with your partner the key word/s you have identified. Then write the answers to the questions in Exercise 6. Compare your answers with your partner's.

 D Vocabulary

8 WAGGGS joined a scheme in 1997 called HARP – the Health of Adolescent Refugees Project – which is being run in three countries: Uganda, Zambia and Egypt. You are going to read about the project. Before you do so, look at these words which have been removed from the text. Discuss each word with your partner and try to agree on a possible meaning. Do *not* use your dictionary yet.

adequate   preferential

compromised   prevalent

counterparts   sanitary

curricula   self-esteem

discriminate   transition

neglects   vulnerable

nutritional

peer

9 Check the meaning of each word from Exercise 8 in your dictionary.

E Reading and writing

10 Skim the text and briefly answer these questions. You do *not* need to write anything.

    a According to the text, what is an adolescent?

    b How many of her peers is each girl expected to reach?

WAGGGS and the HARP project

Adolescents can be a (**1**) group of people as they make the (**2**) to being an adult. Adolescents are neither children nor adults, and as such are often overlooked by existing health programmes. The child–adult transition is made even harder for refugee adolescents because of living in a new place, where they may have no family to give them support and guidance. Refugees may have experienced or witnessed violence and their health may have been (**3**) by poor living conditions, a lack of knowledge about where to go and seek help and the limited number of health workers able to provide (**4**) services.

Furthermore, it is known that adolescent refugee girls are often subject to the same problems as their adult (**5**):
- (**6**) feeding practices customarily (**7**) against girls and women;

- food aid frequently (**8**) the special (**9**) requirements of girls and women;
- health services are often inaccessible to women and adolescent refugees;
- family violence is (**10**);
- safety while seeking water, animal feed and cooking fuel is often lacking;
- (**11**) protection and soap are often unavailable.

HARP provides education on a range of health issues such as nutrition, physical and emotional changes through adolescence, hygiene, preventing disease, and (**12**). Refugee girls and young women learn about these topics through the use of Girl Guide and Girl Scout methods. They create posters, songs, poems and role-plays. They also create a flipbook which contains drawings and explanations of the topics.

There are three (**13**) for different ages, and once the girl has completed the curriculum she gains a badge. Leaders from the local refugee community are trained to be able to deliver the HARP programme.

The second part of the project then challenges each girl to take the messages they have learned out to the local community through (**14**) education. This means that they use the flipbook and the songs, poems and role-plays that they have created to teach their friends about the topics they have covered. Each girl is challenged to reach 25 of her peers. This peer education earns them bronze, silver and gold certificates. Through the network of peer educators, the health messages have the potential to reach 22,500 adolescent girl refugees.

Source: Adapted from http://www.wagggsworld.org/projects/harp/html

11 Read the text in more detail and write down a word from Exercise 8 for each numbered gap. When you have finished, check your answers with your partner.

12 Work with your partner. Each of you should write five questions which relate to factual information in the text. Student A should use the first two paragraphs, and Student B paragraphs three and four. When you have written your questions, give them to your partner, who will answer them. Check your partner's answers.

(F) Writing

13 Read this **exam-type question**. What exactly do you have to do? Discuss with your partner. Do *not* write anything yet.

> You have just spent a day with one of the girls involved in the HARP project. Write an article for your school magazine in which you:
> * describe the girl and where she came from
> * explain what you learned during your day with her
> * suggest ways in which your school and your friends could help HARP
>
> Your article should be about 150–200 words long (100–150 for the Core curriculum).

14 Read this article written by a student in response to the question in Exercise 13.

> The girl I met was named Fatima Jawali and she was aged 17 years old. She came here last week to explain me about the HARP project and the work she is doing there. I learned that she has been doing it for 2 years now and is using many different techniques as books, songs and poems. She works with girls the same age as she is but there are different ages groups as well. When she will complete her work she will to get a badge. She is trained by a local refuge leader. When she will get the badge Fatima will to go to see her friends and explain them about the situation. She will take her books and songs and poems with her face and teach them what she learned. When she will teach 25 friends she will to get a gold certificate.

15 The writer of the article has made some mistakes. With your partner, identify the mistakes, but do *not* rewrite the article. Think not only about spelling and grammar mistakes, but also about whether or not the writer has answered the question. Is anything missing from the answer? Is the layout correct? What about the length? Repetition? Range of vocabulary?

16 Use the notes below to write your own answer to the question in Exercise 13. You may add ideas of your own, but try to include all the information given. Remember that the limit is 150–200 words (100–150 for the Core curriculum).

> * Fatima Jawali, 17, tall, from small village in Uganda, three brothers, two sisters, both parents missing during recent conflicts
> * works with HARP – learns about problems refugees from Zambia and own country face, such as food and hygiene issues
> * started two years ago, uses posters, songs, poems and role-plays
> * creates flipbook which contains everything learned
> * when finished learning will go to friends and educate them using flipbook
> * must try to reach 25 friends
> * richer countries can help by donating funds – maybe book sale at school, or sponsored car wash?

17 Exchange your writing with your partner. Check your partner's work. What should you be looking for?

ⓖ Speaking

18 What do you think about HARP? Do you think it is an effective way to help people who might have lost their family and belongings?

19 What can you as an individual do to help people who are less fortunate than you?

ⓗ Further practice

20 Write a letter to raise funds for a real or imaginary charity. Think carefully about the style and format of your letter, and write about 150–200 words for the Extended curriculum and 100–150 for the Core curriculum.

21 Give an account of a worthy cause or a worthwhile project with which you have been involved. Give details of why you became involved and what role you took. What was the outcome of your participation? Make notes and be prepared to present your account to your class.

22 Find as much information as you can about Guides, Scouts or youth movements in your country. Make notes and be prepared to give a talk to your class about one of the organisations.

23 Read the following article and then answer the questions which follow.

SOMA AKRITON – AN INDEPENDENT YOUTH GROUP

At the beginning of 1998, a group of concerned people in Cyprus decided to set up a new organisation appealing to today's youth. The organisation's objective was to be independent, democratic and modern.

On 14 March 1998, in the Kaimakli area of Nicosia, *Soma Akriton* was established, its main aims being to offer knowledge and new ideas to the youth of Cyprus, to reinforce the ideals of good citizenship, and to raise awareness of environmental issues. Now a flourishing organisation, whose activities are run by an elected council, *Soma Akriton* organises youth groups in the Nicosia area. The groups are selected by age: 6–11 years, 11–15 years, 15–18 years, and over 18 years. Currently there are five groups, with more than 150 children and young people participating in a rich and varied

programme of events during the months of September to June, when the members meet every Saturday afternoon. Each group is directed by a leader and two or three assistants, all of whom have considerable experience in working with children of all ages. The leaders are all university or college graduates, and are people with high ideals and a desire to offer something back to society.

Soma Akriton pursues five areas of interest:

Nature exploration

This involves the search for new areas of physical beauty in the mountains and along the coast of Cyprus with the aid of maps and compasses. Hiking expeditions and survival excursions take place at different times of the year, with a focus on nature study and observation.

Protection of the environment

Raising awareness and campaigning for the protection of the environment is a top priority with *Soma Akriton*. In 2002, a successful campaign against the use of plastic bags was supported by the European Union, and a campaign to encourage a more 'green' approach to consumerism was funded by the United Nations.

Civil defence

Members of *Soma Akriton* are trained to deal with emergencies such as fires, accidents and earthquakes. There are special emergency teams made up of leaders and children who are equipped with first-aid kits and fire extinguishers.

Quality of life

The exploration of Cypriot civilisation with regular visits to archaeological sites, traditional villages and museums is the focus of 'quality of life'. Comparisons are made with other cultures and societies to increase and improve members' understanding of how other people live. Trips to Germany (in 2000) and Italy (in 2002) as well as participation in European Union programmes and events all add to the aims of the quality of life activities.

General knowledge

From the Olympic Games to healthy eating, from philosophers to inventors, from sport to medicine, from games to projects, *Soma Akriton*'s members are guaranteed a wide range of interests and activities, all designed to broaden and develop their general knowledge.

a List the **three** aims of the *Soma Akriton* organisation.

b Who oversees the activities of the organisation?

c How are the 150 members of *Soma Akriton* grouped at the moment?

d What particular qualities should the group's leaders possess?

e What equipment is used on hiking expeditions and survival excursions?

f Which **two** organisations have supported *Soma Akriton*'s efforts to protect the environment?

g How is the civilisation of Cyprus investigated?

Unit 14: *Focus on listening skills*

Exam Part 2

Ⓐ Writing and speaking

1 This unit is going to focus on nurses and nursing: the job, the history of the profession, and so on. On your own, make a list of as many words and phrases as possible connected with nursing, for example *caring, honourable career*.

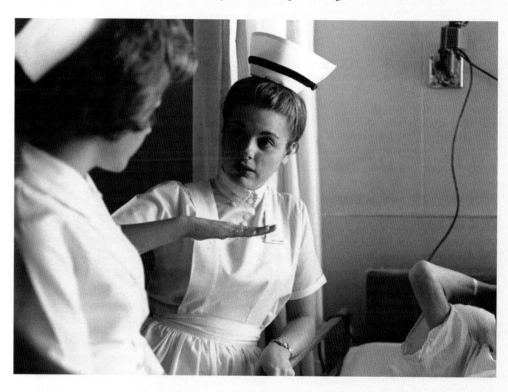

2 Compare your list with your partner's. Are the words and phrases you thought of the same or different?

3 Using some of the words and phrases from Exercises 1 and 2, write a short paragraph in which you describe what qualities you think a nurse should have. Begin like this: 'A nurse should be …' or 'Nurses must have …'. Write about 50 words.

4 Exchange your writing with your partner. Do you agree on the qualities a nurse should have?

5 Florence Nightingale is one of the most famous nurses in history. What do you know about her?

Track 8

B Listening

6 You are going to listen to a radio talk in which a nurse talks about the work Florence Nightingale did. As you listen, make notes about the events which took place in the following years:

a 1820

b 1850

c 1853

d March 1854

e autumn 1854

f November 1854

g 1907

h 1910

7 Compare your notes with your partner's.

8 Listen to the talk again. As you listen, complete the notes below.

> **FLORENCE NIGHTINGALE**
>
> Born: Florence, Italy
>
> As schoolchild, …… and had no problems at school.
>
> Visited homes for sick people, investigated hospitals and …… .
>
> Nursing not considered suitable …… in mid 19th century.
>
> Travelled in Italy, Greece, Egypt and …… .
>
> After training course, started work at …… in London.
>
> FN went to Turkey with …… nurses.
>
> Doctors felt …… by FN and nurses.
>
> FN given a …… in 1907. She became …… in 1895.
>
> Her …… have influenced modern health care.

9 Read the transcript on page 162 and check your notes.

C Reading

10 You are going to read a short text about the Florence Nightingale Foundation. Before you read, think about what a foundation of this sort might do. Why do you think it has been established?

11 The following words and phrases have been removed from the text. With your partner, discuss what they mean. Use your dictionary for help.

**broaden   envisaged   footsteps   founder   memorial
observe trends   pay tribute   universally**

12 Scan the text. Complete each numbered gap with a word or phrase from Exercise 11.

The Florence Nightingale Foundation

Florence Nightingale, who is (**1**) recognised as the (**2**) of modern nursing, died in 1910 at the age of 90. The international nursing community at the time wished to (**3**) to the life and work of this great nurse, and at the International Council of Nurses (ICN) Congress held in Cologne in 1912, it was proposed that an appropriate (**4**) to her should be established. An educational foundation was (**5**), which would enable nurses to prepare themselves to follow in Florence Nightingale's (**6**).

However, due to the 1914–18 war, it was not until 1929 that anything happened, when the Florence Nightingale Memorial Committee was elected. Today, the renamed Florence Nightingale Foundation operates from offices in London, offering nurses the opportunity to (**7**) their professional development through travel to other countries, to (**8**) and work in their own particular area of practice.

If you would like to receive a copy of *A Short History of the Florence Nightingale Foundation*, please write to:

The Florence Nightingale Foundation, Suite 3, 38 Ebury Street London SW1W 0LU.

If you would like more information about her life, visit these links:

http://www.florence-nightingale.co.uk/

http://www.spartacus.schoolnet.co.uk/

http://www.florence-nightingale-foundation.org.uk/

Source: Adapted from http://www.florence-nightingale-foundation.org.uk/historypage.html

13 Compare your answers with your partner's.

14 Read the text again. Before you answer the following questions, find the key word/s in each one.

a When was Florence Nightingale born?

b Why did the international nursing community want to honour the life and work of Florence Nightingale?

c What did the ICN decide to do as a tribute to her?

d What was the purpose of the proposed educational foundation?

e Why was nothing done until 1929?

f Where is the Florence Nightingale Foundation?

g In what ways does the Foundation help nurses?

h How can you obtain more information about Florence Nightingale?

15 Give your answers to your partner to check. Has your partner given a precise answer? Has all the necessary information been included?

D Speaking and vocabulary

16 Look at these two symbols. What do they stand for?
What do the letters ICRC stand for?

17 What types of assistance do you think the ICRC might provide? To whom?
Where in the world would you expect the organisation to be operating?

18 You are going to listen to someone who works for the ICRC being interviewed.
Before you listen, look at these words and phrases taken from the interview.
What do they mean? Discuss with your partner. Use your dictionary for help.

a relief workers   e ethnic   h veterinary care

b victims of famine and drought   f foundations   i priorities

c instability   g hygiene   j waterborne

d insecure

19 Here are some of the questions the interviewer asks. What do you think the
answers might be? Discuss with your partner.

a Can you tell us about how the ICRC assists victims of famine and drought,
and other natural disasters?

b What about health care? Isn't that a priority?

c Does the ICRC only assist when there is a crisis?

d Is it dangerous working for the ICRC?

 E Listening

Track 9

20 Listen to the interview and check your answers to the questions in Exercise 19.

21 Listen to the interview again and complete the notes below.

> **ICRC**
> Number of relief workers: 1,200
> Natural disasters frequently happen at times of other problems such
> as ...... or ....
> Ethnic, political, economic and ...... contexts may create extra problems.
> In the 'Assistance Pyramid', preference is given to ...... and ...... first.
> Medical care takes ...... place.
> Millions of people have problems getting ....
> ...... and ...... are diseases carried by water.
> ICRC relief workers have these qualities: motivated by ...... and can cope
> with ....

22 Check your answers with your partner. If you are unsure, read the transcript
on pages 162–163.

F Speaking

23 What do you know about the ICRC now? Without looking at your notes, tell your partner about the organisation.

24 People who work for the ICRC need to be prepared to leave for any destination in the world at a moment's notice. How would you feel about being in that position? Would you find it exciting or frightening? Why? Do you think you could work for an organisation like the ICRC? Why/Why not? What might be some of the advantages and disadvantages of that kind of life?

25 The ICRC employs people who are mentally mature, motivated and who have potential for personal development. Does that description fit you or anybody you know? Why/Why not? What motivates people who work for the ICRC? Can you think of anyone who might be suited to work for the ICRC?

G Further practice

26 Write a letter to the ICRC informing the Head of Personnel that you would like to be considered as a relief worker. Include in your letter information about your qualifications, as well as your personal abilities. Write 150–200 words.

27 *Student A:* Give a spoken account of a natural disaster which you have experienced, or which you have followed in the news.

Student B: Listen to Student A's account of a natural disaster and make notes of the important points. Then write up your notes into a short summary of about 100 words.

28 Listen to the news in English on the radio or television today. Write two sentences summarising each of the news items you hear, giving factual details of names, places and numbers.

29 Imagine that you want to attend a course leading to a Diploma in Nursing, or a Certificate in First Aid. Copy and complete the application form below.

---

1 PERSONAL DETAILS

COURSE APPLIED FOR: _____

FAMILY NAME: _____   GIVEN NAME: _____

SEX: MALE ☐   FEMALE ☐

DATE OF BIRTH: _____

ADDRESS: _____

_____

_____

POST CODE: _____

HOME TELEPHONE: _____   MOBILE PHONE: _____

EMAIL: _____

2 ACADEMIC BACKGROUND

IS ENGLISH YOUR FIRST LANGUAGE?   YES ☐   NO ☐

IF 'NO' WHAT IS YOUR FIRST LANGUAGE? _____

SCHOOLS ATTENDED:

1 _____

2 _____

LIST ANY CERTIFICATES OR QUALIFICATIONS YOU CURRENTLY HOLD:

_____

_____

_____

_____

PLEASE TELL US WHY YOU WISH TO FOLLOW THE COURSE. DO NOT WRITE MORE THAN ABOUT **100** WORDS.

_____

_____

_____

_____

_____

_____

_____

Unit 15: *Exam practice*

In this unit you will have the opportunity to do some examination practice with exam-type questions. These will focus on the examination areas covered in the previous four units: exam Exercises 1 and 2 (reading), 4 and 5 (reading and writing), and listening.

For information on how you will be assessed in the examination, see Unit 5.

Reading: Exam exercises 1 and 2

1   Here is a notice from a hotel. Study the notice carefully and answer the questions which follow.

ROYALE HOTEL ANSE

Dear Guests

The Royale Hotel Anse in Seychelles is an environmentally-conscious hotel, and is dedicated to the protection of the environment within the travel and tourism industry.

Water – did you know?
- 97% of the Earth's water supply is contained in oceans, and 2% is frozen. This leaves 1% of drinkable water. Wherever you are in the world, it is easy to see that this represents a very limited water supply.
- Showers use 20–30 litres of water per minute.
- Each toilet flush uses about 15 litres of water.
- After drinking a glass of water, we use up to two more glasses of water to wash it.
- Even a small, slow drip from a tap can waste more than 70 litres in 24 hours.
- A running tap uses up to 20 litres per minute. Letting a tap run while brushing your teeth wastes more water than one person needs to drink in a week.

The Royale Hotel Anse is a water-conscious hotel. How?
- Our chefs wash all vegetables with the plug in the sink.
- All water used in the hotel for cleaning and washing is recycled through our water-treatment equipment.
- The hotel gardens are watered using recycled water from the water-treatment equipment.
- All the hotel's taps, pipes, toilets, showers and baths are regularly checked for leaks by our engineers, and immediately repaired if necessary.
- In order to save both water and electricity, dishwashing machines are only switched on when they are full.
- Our staff undergo regular training in environmental issues.

a   How limited is the world's water supply?   **[1]**

b   Which uses more water per minute: a shower or a running tap?   **[1]**

c   What is the result of letting a tap run while you brush your teeth?   **[1]**

d   How do the hotel's chefs save water?   **[1]**

e   When would the hotel's pipes or taps need to be repaired by
    the engineers?   **[1]**

f   Why are the hotel staff water-conscious?   **[1]**

[Total: 6]

2   Here is a doctor's leaflet about how to cope with asthma, a breathing problem.
    Read the leaflet carefully and then answer the questions which follow.

COPING WITH ASTHMA

What is asthma?

In the lungs there are thousands of tiny tubes called 'airways', which distribute air throughout the human body. There are several natural defence mechanisms to protect the lungs against dust and infection, but in people with asthma, these defence mechanisms are over-sensitive. This causes the airways to close, making it difficult to breathe.

People who are susceptible to asthma may have an attack brought on by:

- exercise
- environmental factors (such as cold air, traffic exhaust fumes, smoke, hair from domestic animals)
- situations of strong emotion, especially in children

Who gets asthma?

Asthma seems to be partly inherited and partly caused by environmental factors. Current surveys indicate that about 10–20% of children and 2–5% of adults have asthma. This reflects the fact that asthma often disappears or ceases to be a problem when children grow up, although it may also return in later life. Among children, more girls than boys have asthma, but in adults, men and women are affected equally.

Surveys also show that asthma has increased considerably during the last 30 years in most countries. The cause of this change is not known.

Increases or differences in environmental pollutants could be partly responsible, but many other changes in lifestyle that might affect asthma have occurred during this time.

How is asthma treated?

There are two different types of asthma medication:

Relievers: these re-open the blocked airways during an asthma attack. The medication is inhaled directly into the lungs from an aerosol, which is used whenever it becomes difficult to breathe. Relievers are designed for a rapid effect.

Preventers: these are long-acting medications taken regularly every day to maintain a constant protective effect. They act by reducing the over-sensitivity which allows asthma attacks to start. Most are inhaled, but some are taken as tablets.

How do I get more information?

In many countries there are support organisations and patient groups whose purpose is to give advice and practical help to people with asthma. Ask your doctor, asthma specialist nurse or pharmacist for details.

This leaflet can only give general information about asthma. You should always follow the advice given by your doctor for your individual case.

Source: Adapted from the leaflet 'Coping with Asthma', September 1998

a   What happens to people as a result of having over-sensitive defence mechanisms in the lungs? [1]

b   What could bring on an asthma attack? Name **two** things. [1]

c   What causes asthma? Name **two** factors. [1]

d   What may happen to children who have asthma as they grow up? [2]

e   What might be the cause of the increase in asthma during the past 30 years? [1]

f   Name the **two** types of medication used to treat people with asthma. [1]

g   What are the main differences between the two medications? Name **two**. [2]

h   Give **two** ways in which more information may be obtained. [1]

[Total: 10]

1 Read the following article about some of the islands in the Indian Ocean, and complete the task which follows.

IT'S BETTER IN THE INDIAN OCEAN ...

The Maldives, Mauritius, Reunion, Seychelles

The Maldives came late to international tourism development, and have attempted to avoid many of the negative effects on the local economy and the environment seen in other parts of the world. There are strict controls on the development of resorts, and only certain of the individual islands may be developed for tourism. This, and the fact that the largest island has an area of 13 square kilometres, means that usually a single resort occupies an entire island, becoming effectively a hotel with a beach instead of walls.

Virtually all food apart from fish is imported, and this means that prices are comparatively high. The Maldives have aimed for the top end of the tourist market, and this could be both good and bad: bad because you may not be able to afford to visit; good because, if you can afford to go there, there will not be crowds of tourists going with you.

The Maldives are more sea than land, so there is an abundance of beautiful dive sites, and the country has a well-deserved reputation as one of the best

diving regions in the world. If you want warm water, excellent visibility up to 50 m and an abundance of sea-life, you cannot go wrong.

However, if volcanoes are more to your liking, the volcanic islands of Mauritius and Reunion (both situated about 1,000 km to the east of Madagascar) offer the chance to

explore beautiful beaches and lunar-like landscapes. The central plateau of Mauritius is surrounded by mountains, including Piton de la Rivière Noire (826 m). The beaches, fringed by palm trees, offer a range of activities from snorkelling through the coral reefs to sailing, tennis and volleyball. The climate of both islands is tropical with heavy rains in winter. Sugar-cane plantations cover extensive areas, along with tea and tobacco on Mauritius.

Seychelles, an archipelago of more than 90 islands, is abundant in coral reefs; 40 of the islands are mountainous, and just over 50 are smaller coral islands. Only the largest islands are inhabited, and the economy depends heavily on tourism, which employs about 30% of the workforce. With the tropical climate, there is heavy rainfall but plentiful vegetation.

	Area	Population	Capital
Maldives	298 km²	311,000	Malé
Mauritius	1,860 km²	1,190,000	Port Louis
Reunion	2,510 km²	733,000	St-Denis
Seychelles	455 km²	80,000	Victoria

Source: Adapted from *The Independent on Sunday*, 19 May 2002

You are going to give a talk for a geography project about some of the islands in the Indian Ocean. You have decided to use information from this article in your talk.

To help you plan your talk, **make two short notes under each of the following headings.**

a Maldives: development of tourism [2]

b Maldives: scuba-diving [2]

c Mauritius and Reunion: geography [2]

d Seychelles: the islands [2]

[Total: 8]

2 Read the following article about the origins of pizza. Write a summary explaining:

- the development of pizza up to and including 1858

- the popularity of pizza today

Your summary should be about 100 words long, and you should use your own words as far as possible. You will be given up to 6 marks for relevant points that you make and up to 4 marks for the way in which you write about these points.

PIZZA, PIZZA, PIZZA

The origins of pizza can be traced back to the Romans who baked a type of bread called 'picea'. At the end of the first millennium and the beginning of the second, the name 'pizza' had already become accepted, although the flat, round thing produced from the early medieval oven still looked very like an ordinary flat cake. It was a long time before the genuine Neapolitan pizza with tomato sauce, anchovies, capers and mozzarella came into existence.

A recipe from 1858 describes something much more like the popular food we know as pizza today. This early recipe describes a piece of dough (the pizza 'bread') rolled out into a flat, round shape using a rolling pin or the hands, and covered with any food available, topped with oil, and then baked in an oven. The recipe also lists other ingredients, such as chopped garlic, cheese, herbs, and thin slices of fish. It even mentions that the pizza dough could be folded over in half to make what we now know as pizza calzone, or 'sock' pizza.

For a long time, pizza remained a regional speciality. Other products from the south of Italy spread slowly but surely to the north, but pizza was slower to travel. It first made a detour to New York in the USA where people bought the dough bread with its delicious toppings from street-vendors and

ate it as a snack between meals. The first 'Neapolitan' pizzeria opened in New York in 1905. Sixty years later, pizza had become established not only in the USA, but was also eagerly eaten in northern Europe. It was only in Italy – with the exception of Naples – that pizza remained relatively unknown. This nutritious snack did not make its entrance into Rome and the northern parts of Italy until the 1970s and 1980s.

Today, however, pizza is even mentioned in the *Guinness Book of World Records*. The society of pizza-makers regularly organises competitions in which the most talented *pizzaioli* (pizza-makers) are rewarded not only for unusual creations but also for their sometimes acrobatic skills when throwing the thin, flat cakes of dough into the air and catching them again.

In the 21st century, pizza is eaten all over the world, and has perhaps overtaken spaghetti as our idea of typical Italian food. Even in the most remote towns and villages, there is often somewhere to buy pizza, and in large cities a whole army of pizza delivery restaurants advertise their products. Supermarkets sell all types of frozen pizza in a wide price range, and if you want to try your skills as a *pizzaiolio*, your local market is sure to sell all the necessary ingredients. *Buon appetito!*

Source: Adapted from *Culinaria Italy*, 2000

Listening

Track 10

Listen to the interview about problems with traffic. Then copy and complete the notes below.

You will hear the interview twice.

By 2030: **(1)** ...... *people will be killed on roads in developing countries each year.*

Every day: *3,000 people are* **(2)** ...... *and 30,000 seriously* **(3)** ......

Apart from accidents: **(4)** ...... *claims 400,000 lives each year.*

Levels of pollution monitored by: **(5)** ......

Damage to people will affect: *their health,* **(6)** ...... *potential and the health* **(7)** ...... *of national administrations.*

Statistics from: **(8)** ......

People most at risk: *pedestrians,* **(9)** ...... *,* **(10)** ...... *and children.*

Policy in South America: *bicycle and pedestrian-only routes,* **(11)** ......, *parks built on* **(12)** ...... *land, car-free days.*

Unit 16: *Focus on reading skills*

Exam Exercises 1 and 2

A Speaking and vocabulary

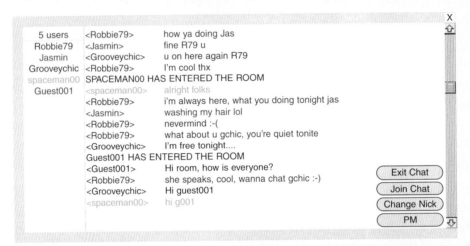

1   What do you think the following symbols and letters mean in internet or mobile phone language? Discuss with your partner. Add to the list any more that you know.

       ☺   ☹   **BFN**   **RU**   **IC**   **LOL**   **L8R**

2   Why do you think people use this language code? What are the benefits of writing 'IC' instead of 'I see' or 'I understand'?

3   What effect do you think that using language codes might have on written language in the future? Do you think it might cause people to write less? Why/Why not? Is it possible that language codes could appear in formal written language? Can you think of any codes which you already use in your writing?

4   You are going to read a newspaper article entitled 'Email sends coded warning to English teachers'. Discuss with your partner what you think the article might be about. Write down **two** points which you think might be in the text.

5   Read the definitions of nine words which have been removed from the text. Match each definition with a word from the list below. Work on your own and do *not* use your dictionary yet.

   a   the short forms of words

   b   developed

   c   messages or letters

d careless, untidy

e the words and phrases used in a language

f to represent, or to be a sign of something

g short, clear, with no unnecessary words

h technical words or phrases

i a possibility that something bad will happen

**abbreviations   concise   evolved   jargon   lexicon
missives   signify   sloppy   threat**

6 Compare your answers with your partner's. Do you agree? Use your
dictionary for help.

 B Reading

7 Scan the text. Identify which of the nine words from Exercise 5 are needed to
complete each numbered gap. Check your answers with your partner.

Email sends coded warning to English teachers

Children are inventing a new (**1**) for electronic communication with a range of (**2**) and symbols that adults find hard to understand. Although educators and politicians were once most concerned about (**3**) pronunciation, it seems that 'email English' poses a greater (**4**) to the language.

For example, the symbol :-(represents a sad face (if you turn your head sideways to look at it) and is widely used to (**5**) sympathy, disappointment or bad news. The symbols have (**6**) to keep down the cost of mobile phone text messages and emailing, speed up the response time and inject emotion into (**7**) (**8**).

Teachers say that the new shorthand style associated with emails is making their job of improving literacy skills even harder. Researchers from the McCann-Erikson advertising agency, who interviewed more

Source: *Cyprus Review*, 8 September 2000

than 100 children aged 5–11, concluded that traditional letter-writing will be of no more use later in life than the history lessons pupils learn in schools.

Robin Laufer, who led the research, said that symbols used in text messages represented new ways of expressing emotions. 'You need intonation if you are going down to the shortest possible form of communication. So if you put a smiley face next to a sarcastic comment, it shows you are joking and not being nasty. We are witnessing a communications revolution which children have adapted to very quickly. Our language is changing in front of our eyes.'

More than half a billion text messages are sent by mobile phone every month. The growing trend coincides with concern over standards in formal writing. Just 54 per cent of 11-year-olds

achieved the expected level in writing in last summer's national tests compared to 78 per cent in reading.

Nigel de Gruchy, general secretary of the NASUWT teachers' union, said that we should now be far more concerned about the influence of email than any failings of teaching. 'Dropping grammar and replacing sentences with (**9**) will damage the language,' he said.

Ms Laufer added: 'Kids have always had some coded language of their own which separated them from grown-ups, but the internet and mobile phones have given them the ability to do this much more. Writing a longhand letter is going to have to be something that is taught at school and, while they will know how to do this, the question is, will they want to?'

8 Check if the two points you wrote down in Exercise 4 are actually in the text.

9 Read the text again and answer the following questions.

   a What do adults find difficult to understand in the new lexicon?

   b What worried people in education before the arrival of 'email English'?

   c What **three** reasons are given for the development of email symbols?

   d According to teachers, what is making their job harder?

   e Why is it suggested that, in the future, traditional letter-writing will no longer be of any use?

   f Why are symbols so important in electronic communication?

   g What does a smiley face symbol represent, according to the text?

   h How many text messages are sent each year?

   i What percentage of 11-year-old children failed to reach the expected level in writing?

   j According to Nigel de Gruchy, what is going to harm the English language?

   k What does Ms Laufer say that the internet and mobile phones have given children?

C Writing

10 According to the text, what are the advantages for young people in using symbols in electronic communication? What do you think people might perceive as the disadvantages? Discuss with your partner and make lists headed 'Advantages' and 'Disadvantages'.

11 *Student A:* Use your notes from Exercise 10 to write a paragraph of about 100 words on the advantages for young people of using symbols in electronic communication.

   Student B: Use your notes from Exercise 10 to write a paragraph of about 100 words on the disadvantages for young people of using symbols in electronic communication.

Vocabulary

12 You are going to read a text about mobile phone technology. Before you read the text, find ten words in the wordbox. Some of the words are horizontal, some vertical, some diagonal, and some are written backwards. All the words appear in the text and are connected with mobile phone technology.

I	N	T	E	R	N	E	T	P	W	E	D	T	Y	T
L	K	E	J	H	G	F	D	S	A	L	M	N	X	V
Z	X	C	C	V	B	N	M	N	E	M	A	E	E	S
E	W	H	Q	E	A	S	D	L	F	G	T	I	G	E
Z	A	N	N	S	X	D	I	G	I	T	A	L	A	G
L	K	O	J	M	N	B	B	G	F	D	D	C	U	A
P	H	L	O	I	O	H	Y	G	T	F	R	D	G	S
S	C	O	M	M	U	N	I	C	A	T	I	O	N	S
Q	G	G	H	I	M	L	P	U	Y	F	D	S	A	E
R	S	Y	M	B	O	L	S	M	B	V	X	Z	L	M

13 Here are definitions for the ten words you found in the wordbox. Match each word with its correct definition. Use your dictionary to check your answers.

  a words for communication

  b can be moved easily

  c computer system which allows people around the world to communicate

  d information in the form of numbers

  e information or facts

  f pictures or shapes which represent a particular meaning

  g scientific methods

  h spoken or written pieces of information

  i ways of sending information

  j written words

E Reading

14 Here are the six paragraphs which form the text. Scan the paragraphs and decide on a logical order for them. Do *not* worry about the numbered gaps in the text at the moment. Check your order with your partner.

Get the msg?

Paragraph A

Musicworld.com has been among the first companies to act upon this potential. Last month, instead of wasting time and money printing information leaflets, it advertised a music festival by sending out text messages to 5,000 people on the day of the event. The venue was packed out within hours.

Paragraph B

One thing is sure: mobile phone technology continues to advance at a frightening pace. 'We will soon be moving on from SMS to mobile (**1**) applications,' says Dave Tonby, managing director of Global mobile internet company. 'For example, soon you will be able to send a picture from a (**2**) camera as a message to a mobile phone.'

Paragraph C

Despite the enormous potential of SMS, there is the question of the effect text messaging is having on schoolchildren's grasp of grammar and (**3**). In an age when 65 per cent of children

aged between 14 and 16 have their own mobile phone or are loaned one by a parent when going out, educationalists fear that the use of so many abbreviations might hamper their command of formal writing. Mobile phone companies respond, however, that new T9 (**4**), which anticipates and corrects the spelling of words in text messages, could have exactly the opposite effect on literacy rates among youngsters.

Paragraph D

According to global telecommunications companies, 'texting', or SMS (Short Message Service) to give it its official title, is expanding at the rate of 1,800 per cent per year. Around half a billion (5) (6) were sent in the UK last month, compared to 50 million during the same period last year. Worldwide, the number of messages sent via (7) phones last month was approximately 8 billion.

Paragraph E

The phenomenon has also found an enormous market in the world of entertainment. 'SMS is here and now for young people,' says Craig Turnbull, editorial director of musicworld.com, a global music (8) site. 'They love it. You can get straight to the point without wasting time.

People realised a long time ago that SMS is the best way to find someone who you are looking for in a crowd, but now the potentials of SMS are really being exploited. It's going to revolutionise marketing.'

Paragraph F

The SMS phenomenon has even evolved its own sub-language, based around a unique lexicon of abbreviations and (9). Within this strange electronic shorthand, phrases are stripped of their vowels and squashed down to a handful of numbers and letters. Within the youth market, texting continues to be a popular means of (10). A survey published earlier this month shows that 81 per cent of 15–24-year-old mobile phone users are using text messages to coordinate their social arrangements.

Source: Adapted from *The Independent on Sunday*, 24 September 2000

15 Scan the text and identify which one of the words in Exercise 12 is needed to complete each gap. Check your answers with your partner.

16 Answer the following questions. First, identify the key word/s in each question.

   a How fast is the use of texting increasing annually?

   b According to the article, approximately how many text messages were sent outside the UK last month (i.e. in August 2000)?

   c What **two** things happen to sentences when they are changed into electronic shorthand?

   d In what way do a large majority of 15–24-year-olds organise their social activities?

   e Why does Craig Turnbull believe that SMS is 'here and now for young people'?

   f How has musicworld.com used text messaging to its advantage?

   g What was the result of musicworld.com's text messaging?

   h Why are people in education worried about the high percentage of children using mobile phones?

   i How do mobile phone companies respond to the criticisms about mobile phones and text messages?

   j What is the future for mobile phone technology?

F Speaking

17 Think about why you do or do not believe that electronic symbols will harm the English language. Be prepared to present your ideas to your class.

18 With your partner, discuss the points you made in the paragraph you wrote for Exercise 11. Try to convince your partner of your point of view.

G Further practice

19 Find out what the following text messages mean:

    a B4UGO   b CUL8R   c UN428LY

20 Write a letter to a friend in which you tell them about text messaging. You should use information from the passages you have read, but you are free to include your own ideas as well. Write about 150–200 words for the Extended curriculum and 100–150 words for the Core curriculum.

21 Read the text 'Internet cars prepare to cruise the web' and answer the questions.

Internet cars prepare to cruise the web

The car radio could be replaced within five years by an intricate system expected to bring the internet to every luxury vehicle. Motorists will get instant access to data without having to take their hands off the steering wheel. Investors who want to check share prices will be able simply to bark the word 'stocks' at their on-board command centre. A robotic voice will supply the answer.

The new unit, no bigger than today's radio/cassette players, will also provide instant traffic updates, and details of the nearest petrol stations, restaurants, hotels and shops. The results of the driver's favourite football teams will be just a command away.

The new form of in-car communication, known as telematics, is being pioneered by Motorola, which created the first car radio in 1929. The firm has unveiled its prototype, which should be available next year. Engineers are still working out initial kinks. But both the company and its competitors are convinced that direction-finding and basic net access will be standard features by 2005. Drivers will be able to speak telephone messages into a console to be delivered to offices, family and friends; they will hear and send vocalised email, page customers, and even download audio books to accompany them on long journeys. After an accident, the word 'hospital' will prompt an on-screen display of the nearest medical facility. Add 'nav' (for navigate) and a robot will provide spoken directions to the accident and emergency unit.

Although early versions are expected to cost £2,000, manufacturers believe that telematics units could quickly become standard, with business-minded motorists paying £20 per month to link up to the net.

Source: Adapted from *The Sunday Times*, 13 August 2000

a   Within how many years does the writer say that motorists will have internet access in their vehicles?

b   What is the size of the internet in-car unit?

c   Give **six** types of information mentioned in the text that motorists will be able to access.

d   When will Motorola's new in-car communication system be available?

e   What benefit will drivers have on long journeys?

f   How will the new system be useful to people who have just had a car accident?

g   How much will it cost to buy and use the new in-car system?

22 Study the map below. You are at point A and a friend in a car with a mobile phone is lost at point B. Give your friend detailed directions to find you at point A.

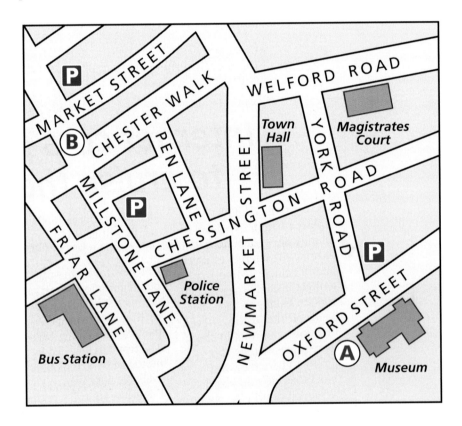

Unit 17: *Focus on reading and writing skills*

Exam Exercises 3, 4 and 5

Ⓐ Speaking and vocabulary

1   Decide with your partner if you think the following statements are true or false. You will have a chance to check your decisions later in this unit.

   a   The North Pole is melting for the first time in 55 million years.

   b   The ocean at the top of the world is one mile across.

   c   The earth is being warmed by fossil fuels.

   d   The average summer thickness of ice at the North Pole used to be about 3 m.

   e   Britain's climate is two or three degrees warmer than that of Greenland.

   f   Britain and the United States have to reduce their greenhouse emissions sharply by 6%–8% in 2012.

   g   America is the world's biggest producer of carbon dioxide.

   h   It is predicted that America will increase its carbon dioxide emissions by 15% over the next 10 years.

   i   The average thickness of polar ice is shrinking by 4% each year.

   j   The North Pole has never before lost its ice.

   k   By 2100, the polar icecap will have melted completely.

2   Look at these newspaper headlines:

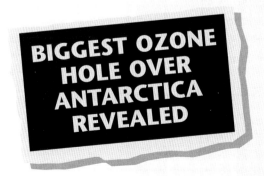

   a   What do you already know about global warming and ozone?

   b   With your partner, make a list of ten things which you know.

   c   Where could you find out more information?

3 Match the words on the left (taken from the text on page 125) with the
   definitions on the right. Check your answers with your partner. If you are not
   sure, use your dictionary for help.

WORDS		DEFINITIONS	
a	shrinking	i	areas of the globe
b	severe	ii	becoming smaller
c	rapid	iii	dirt, things which are unsuitable for human use
d	pollution	iv	is the same as, or follows the same pattern as
e	meltdown	v	process in which something turns from solid to liquid
f	latitudes	vi	serious, worrying
g	fossil	vii	something preserved in rock
h	flourish	viii	to grow well and be healthy
i	consistent	ix	very fast

4 Copy the grid below and write the nine words in Exercise 3 horizontally. If
   you write the words in the correct spaces, the shaded area will reveal the
   name of an area of the globe.

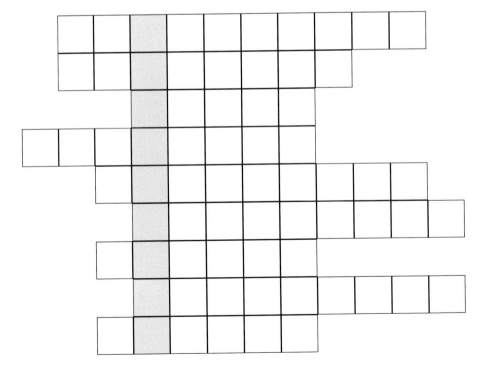

B Reading

5 Skim the text. Which of the three headlines in Exercise 2 do you think is the most suitable for this article? Why?

The North Pole

The North Pole is melting for the first time in 55 million years. Researchers have found that the icecap at the top of the world has turned into a mile-wide patch of open ocean. The melting of the pole last happened on such a scale when the Earth was going through a period of rapid warming. This year's meltdown has been linked with the greenhouse effect, where gases released by burning fossil fuels are trapping ever more heat in the atmosphere and so warming the Earth.

The melting was discovered by James McCarthy, an oceanographer and member of the Intergovernmental Panel on Climate Change (IPCC), which is sponsored by the United Nations to advise the governments on global warming. It coincides with official confirmation that the icecap covering Greenland is also disappearing. Earlier research conducted by McCarthy has shown that the average summer thickness of ice at the North Pole was about 3 metres. This year, however, he was able to take a ship directly to the pole and then had to float over it because there was no ice to stand on. 'It was totally unexpected,' he said.

Researchers had warned that the polar icecap was shrinking by about 6% a year, but nobody had expected the North Pole to melt until global warming had become much more severe. The meltdown could also counteract the Gulf Stream, which keeps Britain's climate two to three degrees warmer than countries at a similar latitude.

The Eocene period, 55 million years ago, was the last time the world's climate grew rapidly warmer. Fossil evidence shows that it became warm enough for tropical vegetation and animals to flourish in the Arctic and Antarctic Circles.

The news comes as the IPCC is drafting an important report on global warming for publication in January. This weekend it emerged that the report will, for the first time, confirm that the Greenland icecap has not only started to melt but also will eventually disappear unless global warming can be halted.

Sir John Houghton, former head of the Meteorological Office, and who now heads the IPCC's scientific panel, said the report would make it clear to governments that the world's climate was changing rapidly. 'We are confident that climate change is due to human activities,' he said.

The news also anticipates the November reopening of negotiations in the Hague over ratifying the 1997 Kyoto climate change agreement. Under the agreement, first world countries such as Britain and the United States of America have to reduce their greenhouse emissions sharply by 6%–8% by 2012. Britain is likely to meet the target but, the report will say, most other countries will fail. America – the world's biggest emitter of carbon dioxide – is predicted to increase emissions by 15%. There is no agreement on reductions after 2012.

Houghton and his colleagues will tell governments that the world must slash greenhouse gas emissions to 60% of 1990 levels by 2050 to avoid the worst

effects of climate change. If the reductions are left for another 50 years, it could prove too late.

The Hadley Centre – the Meteorological Office's climate change unit – has warned of a 'runaway' greenhouse effect where temperatures would reach a point at which it could no longer be stopped. Tony Juniper, campaigns director for Friends of the Earth, said the melting of the North Pole showed how urgently action was needed. 'The melting polar ice is consistent with the predictions of scientists,' he said. 'It shows global warming is for real and governments must agree tougher pollution targets.'

Dr Peter Wadhams, a specialist in sea ice at the Scott Polar Research Institute in Cambridge, said it was wrong to suggest that the North Pole had never lost its ice. 'Polar ice is always moving and these gaps can open up anywhere, including the North Pole. However, it is true that there are now many more of them,' he said. 'Our research shows that the average thickness of the polar ice has reduced by 40% and its area is shrinking by 4% a year. By the end of this century it will have disappeared completely.'

Source: *The Sunday Times*, 20 August 2000

6 Look back at the statements in Exercise 1. Scan the text to find out if you and your partner made the correct decisions.

7 Scan the text again and check if any of the things you already know about global warming and ozone are mentioned. Then, make a list of five more things that you did *not* know. Compare your list with your partner's.

8 Look at the questions in Exercise 9 below. Find the key word/s in each one. Do you and your partner agree?

9 Now answer the questions.

   a When was the last time the North Pole melted?

   b What is the greenhouse effect, according to the text?

   c What did James McCarthy find 'totally unexpected'?

   d What keeps the climate in Britain slightly warmer than other countries in the same area?

   e How do we know that tropical vegetation and animals flourished 55 million years ago?

   f What will happen to the Greenland icecap if global warming is not stopped?

   g According to the IPCC, what is causing climate change?

   h What will happen to the Kyoto agreement after 2012?

   i How can the worst effects of climate change be avoided?

   j What will happen to polar ice during the next 100 years?

10 Exchange your answers with your partner. Check that your partner's answers include all the necessary information. Are there any differences between your answers and your partner's? Discuss and produce final versions of your answers.

ⓒ Writing

11 Look at this **exam-type question**. With your partner, decide exactly what you have to do. What information is asked for? Do *not* write anything yet.

> Read the text 'The North Pole' and then write a summary in which you include information about:
> * the melting of the polar icecap
> * the 1997 Kyoto climate change agreement
>
> You should use your own words as far as possible. Do not write more than about 100 words.

12 Look at this answer to the question in Exercise 11 written by an IGCSE student. After you have read it, decide with your partner if you think it is a good answer to the question. Be prepared to say why. Think about the content of the answer, as well as spelling and grammar.

> Scientists have discovered that the North Pole icecap has melted and become a mile-wide area of sea. The melting is due to the greenhouse effect which warms the Earth. Research showed that the thickness of ice at the North Pole was about 3 metres, but now it is possible to sail a ship directly over the pole. At Kyoto it was agreed that developed countries would have to decrease greenhouse emissions by 8% before 2012. It is expected that Britain will be able to achieve this, but many other countries, including the USA, will not.
>
> (95 words)

13 Look at this **exam-type question**. Read it carefully, then copy and complete the notes.

> Read the text 'The North Pole' and then complete the notes which follow.
>
> **The North Pole**
> a   Melting discovered by ......
> b   Current job ...... and member of IPCC
> c   Early research indicated ice thickness was ...... but this year able to take ship to North Pole and float over it
> d   Gulf Stream keeps Britain's climate ...... warmer than other countries at similar latitude
> e   IPCC report confirms that ...... will eventually disappear if global warming does not stop
> f   Kyoto agreement states that developed countries must ...... by 2012
> g   After 2012 there is ......
> h   To avoid worst effects of climate change governments must ......

D **Speaking and vocabulary**

14 The following phrases appear in the next text you are going to read. What do you think the text is about?

'The dusty wasteland stretching out …'

'… disappear into the burning wind.'

'… the water is no good.'

'… the water table has gradually been drained …'

'… die in the heat.'

'… when the rains return.'

15 With your partner, make a list of ten more phrases or single words which you think you might find in the text. Later you will be able to check if the words you think of are actually in the text.

16 Look at these words and phrases taken from the text. Discuss each one with your partner and try to agree on its meaning. Use your dictionary for help.

**barren   conserve   dislocation   drought   outskirts
play down   sporadic   swaths**

E **Reading**

17 Skim the text. Were your predictions in Exercises 14 and 15 correct? Do *not* worry about the gaps at the moment.

Walk for water grows longer

The dusty wasteland stretching out from the villages is brown and (**1**). 'These are our fields,' said Jay Salaya, a cattle farmer, pointing in despair. 'This is where we usually grow our crops and that is for the cows and buffaloes.' But there are no crops and cattle. In the village of Bead, on the (**2**) of Jamnagar in western Gujarat state, the cakes of soil crumble in your hands and disappear into the burning wind.

On the other side of the village, women dressed in the brightest red, gold and green saris lower black plastic bags on ropes over a brick wall to try to scoop up what is left of the water. 'That well is 100 years old,' said Mr Salaya. 'It is the only one for the village but now the water is no good. It is too dirty. We haven't had enough rain here for three years. The government started to build a water tank for us five years ago but it was never done.'

(**3**) conditions, or prolonged periods of dryness leading to crop failure, are affecting close to 80 million people in 11 states, the government said in a report published last week. The worst hit areas are here in Gujarat and in nearby Rajasthan, both on the border with Pakistan.

India's Prime Minister has announced a 9.5 billion rupee ($214 million) relief package and asked for public donations to help. But he faces growing criticism over his government's failure to predict and prepare for the worsening crisis. For the farmers, the drought came as no surprise. They have been warning of impending water shortages in the worst affected areas for more than six months. It has not rained in Rajasthan or in some areas of Gujarat for three years. As a result, the water table has gradually been drained, and only limited monsoon rains are forecast.

For drinking water the villagers around Jamnagar rely on a government tanker that stops nearby two or three times a week and empties water into a trough. As dusk falls crowds of people walk towards the town to meet the tanker. Some carry tin pots on their heads, while others tie bags to their bicycles.

Farmers walk all day to find water for their cattle. The animals are thin, their hides stretched tight over their bones. 'We have to walk or go by bicycle to get our water,' said Bindi, a sixteen-year-old girl living in a nearby village. 'Sometimes it takes one or two hours. What else can we do? Many of the people are going to the city to look for water.'

Government officials have tried to (**4**) the effects of the drought, which is bringing drastic economic and social (**5**) to the lives of millions of farmers, who have been forced to sell their cattle or watch them die in the heat. There is a division of wealth in this drought. From the air it is clear that whole (**6**) of Gujarat's land have been baked brown. But there are (**7**) pockets of green, signalling areas owned by private farmers wealthy enough to afford their own deep boreholes to keep their crops alive. Gujarat is a vital agricultural supplier, producing a third of India's cotton and peanuts, as well as grain, oilseed, maize, sunflowers and sugarcane.

So far the water shortage has not hurt the towns. Jamnagar is still crowded with traffic, its fruit and vegetable markets are still full of produce, and the Apollo Circus is in town. But the city's beautiful Ranmal Lake, which surrounds the small Lakhota Palace, is dry. Teams of workers, using private and state funds, have been digging the lake deeper, hoping it will (**8**) more water when the rains return. 'If the monsoon rains do not come then there will be trouble for Jamnagar city as well,' said Satesh, a shopkeeper.

Rory McCarthy

Source: *The Guardian Weekly*

18 Scan the text to check if the words you thought of in Exercise 15 appear.

19 Scan the text again and identify which one of the words from Exercise 16 is needed to complete each gap. Check your answers with your partner.

20 Answer the following questions. Then give your answers to your partner to check.

   a Give **two** reasons why Jay Salaya is in despair.

   b What **two** things happen to the soil in the village of Bead?

   c What is wrong with the water in the well?

   d In what **two** ways is the government giving financial assistance?

   e Why were the farmers not surprised by the drought?

   f Where do the villagers around Jamnagar get their drinking water from?

   g How do the villagers carry their water?

   h What evidence is there that some farmers have enough water?

   i What evidence is there that the towns are so far unaffected by the drought?

   j Why have workers been making Ranmal Lake deeper?

  Writing

21 Read the following **exam-type question**. Decide with your partner exactly what you have to do. Do *not* write anything yet.

> Read the article about the drought in Gujarat. Then, using the information in the article, write a summary about how the villagers and farmers of Jamnagar obtain their drinking water. You should not write more than 100 words. You should use your own words as far as possible.

> ! EXAM TIP
>
> The summary question will direct you to a specific topic in the text, so it is very important that you underline the key points and make brief notes before you write your answer.

22 Re-read the text and note the points which relate directly to the summary question in Exercise 21. Then make brief notes. Compare your notes with your partner's. Have you chosen the same information? Has your partner included anything that you have not?

23 Write your answer to the summary question above, paying particular attention to the advice given in this and previous units. When you have written your paragraph, exchange it with your partner. Check your partner's writing. What should you be looking for?

⑥ Speaking

24 Does your country have enough water? Where do you get your drinking water from? Are there any restrictions on how much water you can have?

25 What do you think it would be like to live in a village like Bead, which has so little water? What problems would you face? Do you think that you would be able to cope? Why/Why not?

⑪ Further practice

26 Look again at the text 'Walk for water grows longer'. Write a paragraph of about 100 words outlining what particular problems farmers in Gujarat state are having as a result of the drought.

27 Find out as much as you can about the water supply in your country: where it comes from, how much it costs, if it is chemically treated or not, etc. Prepare a short talk of about 2–3 minutes to give to your group.

28 Design a leaflet informing people in your area of a water shortage and advising them on how to conserve water. You may include pictures and graphics if you wish. Do not write more than about 150–200 words for the Extended curriculum and 100–150 words for the Core curriculum.

29 Read the text 'A dangerous thirst' and then complete the notes on the next page. Write two or three notes under each heading.

A dangerous thirst

We are told that we should drink at least two litres of water a day, and more if we are exercising, but what many people do not realise is that too much water can be fatal. The result is hyponatraemia – literally 'low salt' – a condition also known as 'water intoxication'. When we sweat, we lose vital salts which the body needs to maintain its equilibrium. Excessive sweating combined with drinking dilutes the concentration of salts in the body to a dangerous level. The result is nausea, apathy, lethargy, dizziness and mental confusion; sufferers can lapse into a coma and die.

Hyponatraemia was first noticed in 1981 by a doctor in South Africa when he treated a woman running a marathon. However, anyone is susceptible if they drink water for a prolonged period without ingesting salts.

There are four main factors that could predispose someone to suffer from hyponatraemia. Those most at risk are the very young and the very old, because they are less able to regulate their thirst, and their water and salt levels by themselves. Secondly, anyone who exercises for a prolonged period is at risk; this includes marathon and triathlon competitors. However,

it is not the elite athletes who are in danger, but those who run marathons for charity, or as an occasional hobby. You do not have to be especially fit to suffer from hyponatraemia.

Thirdly, heat and humidity increase susceptibility as sweat loss rises to a litre an hour. The kind of heat at which hyponatraemia can set in is not particularly hot – 20°C. The highest number of incidents recorded at one time was when 24 runners were hospitalised during a marathon in California when the temperature was only 23°C. As it gets hotter, runners slow down but drink more, and do not replace any lost salts.

Drinking more than a litre an hour for five or more hours can lead to hyponatraemia.

Lastly, people in nightclubs are also at risk because the atmosphere is hot and humid, and they tend to stay there for a long time without eating anything but drinking excessive quantities of water. A young woman was recently admitted to hospital after drinking ten litres of water while exercising in a gym. It took the hospital staff about two hours to diagnose her condition, by which time the young woman was unconscious. Her salt levels were found to be dangerously low, and she spent four days in hospital recovering.

Of course, we should all drink water, and we need more during hot and humid conditions but it is best to have drinks with carbohydrates in them, such as squash, and to take sports drinks when exercising.

Source: Adapted from *The Times*, 28 August 2001

Results of hyponatraemia:

- apathy and lethargy

-

-

People at risk:

-

-

-

Advice about drinking water:

-

-

-

Unit 18: *Focus on writing skills*

Exam Exercises 6 and 7

 Ⓐ Speaking

1 Do you chew gum? When? Why? What do you think chewing gum is made from? Do you think it is good for you?

2 Which of the following statements about chewing gum do you think might be true? Decide with your partner.

   a The ancient Greeks chewed a type of gum more than 2,000 years ago.

   b The first manufactured chewing gum was available in 1870.

   c Bubble gum became available in 1928.

   d In the 1950s, the first sugarless gum was produced.

   e Powdered sugar is used to stop pieces of gum from sticking to machinery and packaging.

   f In the USA, 180 sticks of gum is the average consumption per person per year.

   g It is illegal to manufacture, import, or sell gum in Singapore.

   h Turkey is the country with the most gum-manufacturing companies.

   i The Portuguese for chewing gum is *pastilka elastika*.

3   In fact, all of these statements are true. Does anything surprise you? Why/Why not? Why do you think that Singapore has such strict laws about chewing gum? What do you think is the average consumption of chewing gum per person per year in your country?

B Writing

4   With your partner, use the nine statements in Exercise 2 to write a paragraph of information about chewing gum. Do not try to include *all* the information, only that which you consider to be the most important or interesting. Do not write more than 100 words. Remember to use your own words as far as possible.

5   Exchange your writing with another pair. Check their writing. What should you be looking for?

C Speaking and vocabulary

6   You are going to read an article called 'Gum disease'. What do you think the text might be about? Choose from the following:

a   the health dangers of chewing gum

b   the ways in which chewing gum pollutes the environment

c   the benefits of chewing gum

d   how chewing gum is manufactured

7   Work with your partner to decide on the meaning of the following words taken from the text. Use your dictionary for help.

**blight   culprits   defacers   discarded   dislodging
draconian   envisage   hideous   lingers   urging**

8   Here are the first sentences of each of the four paragraphs in the text you are going to read. With your partner, decide in which order you think these sentences should be.

a   City councils throughout the land are trying to cope with the problem.

b   In Birmingham a head teacher has banned chewing gum in her school.

c   Our cities are becoming more beautiful – if you look up at the skyline.

d   The Tidy Britain Group has, in the past two years, been trying out educational campaigns, with the financial support of Wrigleys, the chewing gum manufacturer.

9   Discuss with your partner what you think the whole article is going to be about. Do you think the article will be persuasive or descriptive? Why? Use the sentences from Exercise 8 to help you.

D Reading

10 Scan the text and check your answer to Exercise 6. Do *not* worry about the numbered gaps at the moment.

Gum disease

Paragraph A

(…) If you look down at your feet, however, they are growing more (**1**) every day. Wherever people gather, the pavements are covered with black spots, often dribbling at the edges, like a disease. They are lumps of (**2**) chewing gum that have stuck hard to the pavement and then have been trampled by thousands of dusty soles into black limpets.

Paragraph B

(…) Many have 'gumbuster' machines that spray hot or cold water under high pressure on the spots and, to do them justice, do have some success in (**3**) the ghastly mess. In Edinburgh, these machines are concentrated in areas near nightclubs, schools and roadside seats: the haunts of young people, who are the leading (**4**) of the pavements. For the city's flights of steps, Edinburgh also uses a trigger spray that shoots out a citrus-based oil to break down the gum. These methods are labour-intensive and slow, however, and 'reinfection' is rapid. In the City of Westminster in London, the hot-water machines are out every night. In crowded streets it is not practicable to use them during the day, since the water sprays all round. But Westminster is trying out a steam-cleaning machine that can be used during the day and plans a new assault on the pavement (**5**). Even when the gum is removed, the disease (**6**) – white patches are left where the black spots were previously. For the gum takes with it some of the accumulated dirt and even the surface of the pavement. In Edinburgh, the pavement slabs are cleaned after the gum limpets are removed, but nothing seems to stop the black blotches returning.

Paragraph C

(…) The Mayor of Galway has described his townsfolk as 'filthy people' for the way that they blacken the streets with chewing gum. In Dublin, some firms have called for a ban on the sale of chewing gum in the city centre. Singapore has employed more (**7**) measures. Spitting out gum here can cost (**8**) a fine of S$10,000 (£380). In Britain, it is, of course, an offence to throw down litter – in London the maximum fine is £25. But nowhere have litter wardens proved a success. It is difficult to grab people in the street and to fine or prosecute them, even if they throw down half a burger – and as for chewing gum, how often do you even see people dropping it? Very rarely, though you know they must be doing it all the time. Special bins for gum have been proposed, but as things are, it is difficult to (**9**) teenagers using them. In any event, the gum needs to be wrapped in paper before being put in a bin, otherwise it sticks to the inside and is just as hard to remove as it is to clean it off the pavements.

Paragraph D

(…) In Derby and Birmingham, big adverts were placed in the newspapers and in schools (**10**) children not to throw their gum down. The result was a 50 per cent drop in gum pollution. Last year a similar campaign in the Midlands registered a 30 per cent improvement. (In case you are wondering how anyone knows, researchers counted the spots.) The Tidy Britain Group approach seems the most promising, but will the message stick? Wrigleys, after all, might wish to see the bad effects of chewing gum reduced, but it can hardly be expected to stop making gum. Moreover, many dentists think that sugar-free gum is good for the teeth – it promotes saliva, which helps to wash out the mouth. And anti-smoking groups would rather see people chewing than smoking. Nevertheless, around 20 million people chew gum in Britain, according to Wrigleys. This means vast efforts are needed to tackle the mess they leave behind. Otherwise the new millennium could well be remembered as the spotty millennium.

Source: Adapted from *The Times*, 12 July 2000

11 Scan the text again and identify which one of the words from Exercise 7 is needed to complete each gap. Then, decide where the missing sentences from Exercise 8 should go in the article.

12 Answer the following questions.

    a Why does the writer describe our cities as 'hideous'?

    b Why are the gumbuster machines used near nightclubs and schools?

    c What two methods are used to remove chewing gum from city pavements and steps?

    d Why can't the water sprays be used during the day?

    e What additional problem results from the removal of chewing gum from pavements?

    f Why have litter wardens not proved successful in catching people dropping litter?

    g What reasons are given for not introducing chewing gum litter bins?

13 Give your answers to your partner to check. Then, work with your partner to produce combined answers.

 E Writing

14 Look at this **exam-type question**. With your partner, decide exactly what you have to do. Do *not* write anything yet.

> Here are some views about chewing gum expressed by students you know:
>
> 'Chewing gum looks grown-up and cool.'
>
> **'I chew gum when I feel hungry.'**
>
> 'Dropping gum on the street is a very dirty habit.'
>
> *'All my friends chew gum, so I do as well.'*
>
> Write an article for a newspaper or magazine aimed at young people, giving your opinion about chewing gum. The comments above may give you some ideas, but you are free to use any ideas of your own. Your article should be about 150–200 words long for the Extended curriculum and 100–150 for the Core.

In Exercises 6 and 7 you may be asked to write your opinion about something in the form of a newspaper article, or perhaps for your school newsletter or magazine. Usually you will be given help in the form of a list of ideas or other people's opinions, but you do not have to use them in your answer. You are free to use your own ideas, but make sure you keep to the topic. You must show the examiner that you can use the English language for a specific purpose, and that you can organise your ideas in a logical way.

15 What do you think the format of your answer should be? How many paragraphs should it include? Do you need an introduction and a conclusion? Why/Why not?

16 How should you organise the content of your article? What exactly should each paragraph include? Make notes about what is needed.

17 Use your notes and ideas from the previous exercise to write the introduction and conclusion to your article. Make sure that you state your purpose in writing the article, and restate your main opinion about the subject at the end.

18 Read your partner's two paragraphs. What do you think? Has your partner given a reason for writing and restated their main opinion in the conclusion?

19 Now write the 'body' of the article. Think carefully about how many paragraphs you need to express your opinions. Remember the word limit.

 F Reading

20 Read the article 'A little pick-me-up for the consumer boom's outcasts'. As you read, identify a maximum of ten words which you are not sure about, and which may prevent you from understanding large parts of the article. It is not important to understand everything that you read.

A little pick-me-up for the consumer boom's outcasts

Sit outside one of the hypermarkets that ring Budapest, and you can watch a stream of shoppers rattling their carts through the automatic doors, or stopping for an ice-cream as they emerge laden with goodies. It is possible to get almost anything you want in Hungary these days – exotic fruits that were unknown a few years back, cheese from all over Europe, and a dazzling choice of foreign dishwashers, refrigerators and cookers. If you have enough money, that is.

But a lot of people do not. A surgeon friend showed us his pay slip the other day. His high-stress job in a casualty department is worth just over $170 a month, so he works on Saturday nights as a disc jockey to support his wife and two-year-old son. Others are even less fortunate. Budapest is enjoying a construction boom, and the government reported a sharp fall in unemployment last month. But there has been no obvious decline in the number of homeless people roaming the streets, and unemployment is sure to soar again this winter.

So the annual *lomtalanitas* (collection of unwanted items), when people turn out their basements and dump the contents at the side of the street for the council to take away, is still a keenly awaited event. The day before the pick-up for their district people get up early to put their stuff on the pavement before going to work. Then there's almost a party atmosphere as neighbours sort through discarded beds, mattresses, wash-basins, toilet bowls and tyres in case there's something they need.

The Gypsies and scrap metal dealers are up early too. 'Got the other one, dearie?' a Romany woman asks a man who is dumping a bedside table outside a block of flats. Another resident grabs a bed almost before its previous owner has put it down, carries it upstairs and re-emerges with a smaller one.

The basement of our house in the southwestern district of Kelenfold has not been emptied for a decade, and the family descends on us at 7 am to weed out the treasures of yesteryear, when you threw nothing remotely serviceable away in case there was a sudden shortage, or someone got married and needed to fix a bathroom or a kitchen in their new home.

One by one these dusty trophies emerge: a bent tandem bicycle frame, a chipped sink, a divan with faded green upholstery, a collection of old tyres from the family car, which is still in service. Under the eagle eye of my mother-in-law, Edit, who uses her veto several times because she cannot bear to part with something, we lug the stuff up the stairs and across the grass of the little park to a growing pile of similar objects.

The tandem does not stay there long. Three scrap dealers lurking at the edge of the pile pounce on it, and one of them takes it to a van. A second attacks the sink with a blunt object, to free the taps and metal piping attached to it. The third inspects a loo contributed by a neighbour.

On the whole it is all very polite and good-humoured. One of the scrap men actually asks if it is OK to remove a child's two-wheeler. But across the way an elderly resident bawls out a ponytailed hippie who tries to put a small wooden something or other on a second heap. 'That's my pile,' shouts the older man, arguing that the object contravenes regulations (the *lomtalanitas* does not include ordinary household refuse or debris from building sites). Ponytail slinks off, to return later with a larger wooden object that he deposits on our pile alongside some sticks contributed by an old woman from a house opposite.

Our basement cleaned out, we set off in the car, past 20 or 30 battered fridges neatly stacked on some waste ground. As we drive by, a tiny pick-up truck approaches with two more. People are always looking for a fridge that works: these will be cannibalised, and the better-looking ones sold.

When we get home late in the afternoon the heap on our side of the park stretches for 25 metres along the street and 15 metres on the grass. At its highest it rises a good 3 metres. A few latecomers are nosing gloomily around in case the professionals have left anything worth having. Their task seems pretty hopeless. But these outcasts of the consumer boom have learned to make even a forlorn hope go a long way.

David North

Source: *The Guardian Weekly*, 28 September 2000

21 Compare the words you chose with your partner's. Did s/he choose the same words as you? Together, try to work out the meaning of your words. If you need help, use your dictionary.

G Speaking

22 What do you think about the *lomtalanitas* method of disposing of things that are no longer needed? Would it work in your country? Why/Why not? Can you think of a better way of getting rid of unwanted household things? Discuss your ideas with your partner.

23 What do you think might happen without the system described in the article?

H Writing

24 Look at this *exam-type question*. Do *not* write anything yet.

> Your town has received a sum of money to improve its facilities for the disposal of household rubbish and unwanted goods. Write an article for your local newspaper saying how you think the money should be used, and why. The comments below may give you some ideas but you are free to use any ideas of your own. Your answer should be about 150–200 words long (100–150 for the Core curriculum).
>
> 'We need to spend the money on providing more waste disposal units.'
>
> *'The council should buy trucks which can go to houses to collect large items of rubbish.'*
>
> 'Schools need to educate children about the benefits of recycling.'
>
> *'The money could be better spent in building a new hospital.'*

25 Consider exactly what you have to do and plan your answer accordingly. Think about how much time you should spend on planning. Make notes for each of your paragraphs. Remember that this question asks you to give *reasons* for your decisions.

26 Write your article. Give your article to your partner to read and check.

① Further practice

27 Answer the following **exam-type question.**

> Technology plays an important part in our lives. Write an article for your school magazine in which you explain how you think technology will affect your life during the next 20 years. Your article should be 150–200 words long (100–150 words for the Core curriculum).

! EXAM TIP

Although you do not have much time for planning, you should underline the key word/s in the question to make sure you do exactly what is asked. Write very brief notes, putting your ideas into a logical order. Check for repetition. When you have finished your answer, check your spelling, grammar and punctuation.

28 Re-read the text 'A little pick-me-up for the consumer boom's outcasts' and answer the following questions.

 a What does the surgeon do in order to increase his salary?

 b Why has the country experienced a fall in the number of people being out of work?

 c Why is the annual *lomtalanitas* eagerly awaited?

 d When do people put their unwanted things outside their houses?

 e Why did people in the past not throw anything away?

 f What did someone remove from the sink?

 g Give two examples of things which are not allowed in the *lomtalanitas*.

 h What will happen to the 20 or 30 fridges?

 i Why is the task of the latecomers hopeless?

29 Most schools ban the use of chewing gum. In the role of a teacher, give a short talk on why it is unacceptable to chew gum in schools. Consider not only pollution and health, but also the attitude that chewing gum can convey to others.

30 Television has been described as 'chewing gum for the eyes'. What do you think this statement means? Do you agree or disagree? Why? Write your response in about 150–200 words.

Unit 19: *Focus on listening skills*

Exam Part 3

A **Speaking**

1 What is fashion? Does it affect you in a positive or negative way? Is it only clothes which are fashionable? What about furniture? Food? Mobile phones? Cafés? Opinions? Holidays? What do you consider to be fashionable nowadays?

2 What was fashionable when your parents and grandparents were young? Is there anything which you consider still fashionable today? What type of things remain in fashion? What do you understand by the term 'classic'? Have you seen it used in advertising?

3 How do you think fashion will change in the next five years? 20 years? 50 years?

4 You are going to listen to a clothes designer being interviewed on the radio. Before you listen, decide if the following statements are true or false.

   a The clothing industry is backward.

   b Clothes are made in more or less the same way as they were 2,000 years ago.

   c The Jeane Company (famous for its jeans), GHK Electrics (famous for its electronics) and Giovanni Conte (famous for his designs) are collaborating on technical clothing.

   d The first Jeane Company jeans were sold in 1874.

   e One day all clothes will contain micro-computers.

5   All the statements above come from the radio interview you are going to listen to. Does this surprise you? Why/Why not?

6   Look at statement c again. What do you and your partner think might be the result of the Jeane Company/GHK/Conte collaboration? What will technical clothing look like? What do you think the technical clothing will actually do?

Track 11

Listening

7   You will hear the following words in the interview. What do they mean? Discuss with your partner and check in your dictionary.

fibre   spin   thread   weave   cloth

8   Read the questions below and identify the key word/s in each one. Decide exactly what information is being asked for. Discuss with your partner.

a   What has changed about clothing over the years?

b   How many basic stages are there in the clothes-making process?

c   What roles do the three partners have?

d   Where in the new jackets will the earphones be?

e   What will happen when the phone rings?

f   How are the phone and the MP3 player controlled?

g   Where does Conte get the ideas for his clothes from?

h   What type of garments form the majority of Conte's collection?

i   What does Conte hope to include in his future designs?

j   What would be the **two** benefits of face-recognition cameras?

k   Why do you think the interviewer asks if Conte's designs will look fashionable?

9   Now listen to the radio interview and answer the questions in Exercise 8.

10 Listen to the interview again and check your answers. If you need more help you can read the transcript on pages 163–164.

11 Did anything in the interview surprise you? Were your predictions in Exercise 6 correct?

C **Writing**

12 Look at this **exam-type question**. Discuss with your partner exactly what you have to do. Do *not* write anything yet.

WIN A TECHNO-JACKET!

First prize: GHK/Jeane Company/Conte jacket with built-in phone and MP3 player!

To enter the competition: Write an article telling us WHY you would like to win the techno-jacket, and HOW it would be useful to you.

Send entry to: Techno-Jacket Competition, PO Box 29285, Nicosia, Cyprus

You have seen this advertisement in a newspaper for a competition to win a techno-jacket. You have decided to enter. Write an article in which you:

- give your reasons for wanting to win the jacket
- explain how you would use the technology in the jacket
- say why you deserve to win the prize

Your article should be about 150–200 words long (100–150 words for the Core curriculum).

---

13 Work on your own. Make notes for each of the three sections. Remember that this is a competition and therefore your ideas need to be imaginative and interesting. Compare your notes with your partner's.

14 When you are satisfied with your planning, write your entry together with your partner. Do *not* write your name!

15 Your teacher will give you copies of all the entries from your class. With your partner, read all the entries and decide which one should win the prize. Be prepared to say why.

 D **Listening**

Track 12

16 You are going to hear a talk about bespoke shoes. (You will find out what 'bespoke' means when you listen.) Before you listen, read the questions below and identify the key word/s in each one. Decide exactly what information each question is asking for. Discuss with your partner.

a What exactly are bespoke shoes?

b To which **two** things does the speaker compare bespoke shoes?

c How many companies in London make bespoke women's shoes?

d Give **three** ways in which the speaker describes the premises of the shoe companies.

e Why are bespoke shoes made in the same way as they were 100 years ago?

f How many times must the client visit the shoemaker?

g What happens during the first fitting?

h What is a 'last'?

i Why has the design of bespoke shoes not changed?

17 Listen to the talk by a journalist on bespoke shoes and answer the questions in Exercise 16. Make sure you include all the necessary information.

18 Give your answers to your partner to check. Check your partner's answers. What should you be looking for? Use the transcript on page 164 to check your answers.

E   Reading

19 You are going to read a text, but before you read, look at the following list of words and phrases taken from it. What do you think the text is going to be about?

auditions

commercials

exotic location

fashion-dominated

make-up artist

photo shoot

supermodel

20 Skim the text and decide which word or phrase from Exercise 19 is needed to complete each gap.

Style Check programme winner stops in Seychelles

The latest winner of the *Style Check* TV programme in India will be in Seychelles next week for a (**1**) which forms part of her winning package.

Style Check is the (**2**) programme of the MTV channel which is the leading music and youth channel around the world. *Style Check* is watched by people in over 25 million homes twice a week.

Based largely on the very successful show *House of Style*, hosted by Cindy Crawford, *Style Check* is hosted by Malaika Arora, an actress and (**3**). The show is basically like a fashion magazine on TV, bringing fashion off the catwalk and out on to the streets. It also features profiles about people and designers – anything and everything connected with style and fashion.

The main component of *Style Check* is 'Model Mission', a contest run for young people who want to be models. They go through a series of (**4**) and the winner is then flown to an exotic location to be photographed by a fashion photographer.

The winner of the latest competition will be accompanied to Seychelles by an MTV crew, a stylist/designer, (**5**), fashion photographer and supermodel Malaika Arora.

Past winners, namely Valuscha, Udita and Laxmi, are big names in the industry today and are featured extensively in fashion magazines and (**6**). The contest receives hundreds of entries as it is one of the only ones dedicated to model hunts on television in India and all past winners have been a huge success in the business.

In the past, Goa and Rajasthan in India and Sri Lanka have been given the chance to be featured in the show but this year Seychelles has been chosen as the (**7**) for the filming of the show and the photo shoots.

Source: Adapted from: http://www.seychelles-online.com.sc/archives/120110502.html, November 2003

21 Look at the text in more detail and answer the following questions.

a   Where will the latest *Style Check* winner be photographed?

b   How many people watch *Style Check*?

c   Apart from presenting *Style Check*, what other jobs does Malaika Arora have?

d   How is the winner of 'Model Mission' chosen?

e   Apart from the MTV crew, how many other people will go to Seychelles with the winner?

f   In which countries, other than Seychelles, has the photo shoot taken place?

F Speaking

22 In this unit you have listened to people talking about the future of fashion and the traditional way of producing bespoke shoes. You have also read about a TV fashion competition. Think back to how you responded to the question in Exercise 3. Do you still think the same? Has anything you have heard changed your mind? Discuss with your partner.

G Further practice

23 You recently visited a bespoke shoemaker. Write a report on your visit, to be published as an article in a magazine for teenagers. You may use information from the talk you listened to, as well as your own ideas. In your report you should:

- describe where you went and who you met

- explain what you saw and what you learned

- give your opinion about bespoke shoes compared with modern fashions

Your report should be 150–200 words long for the Extended curriculum and 100–150 words long for the Core curriculum.

24 Your entry for the competition in Exercise 12 was given first prize and you won the techno-jacket! Prepare a short talk in which you outline the advantages and disadvantages of owning such a jacket.

25 Find a fashion picture in a magazine and prepare a short talk for your class. Describe the clothing and then give your opinion on its practicality and desirability. Would you want to wear an outfit like this or be seen with someone dressed in one? Why/Why not?

26 Design a garment for the future. Label your design. Write a description giving details of the fabrics and colours, and explaining the purposes and advantages of your design.

4

Unit 20: *Exam practice*

In this unit there is a complete practice examination. Your teacher will advise you which exercises you should do.

Exam exercise 1

Read the following information about food additives, and then answer the questions.

FOOD ADDITIVES

The food industry spends about $20 billion per annum on chemical food additives to improve the colour, flavour, texture and shelf life of its products. On the one hand, these additives protect consumers from food poisoning and prevent food from deteriorating; but on the other hand, the additives change the colour, flavour, surface appearance and texture of food products, and are therefore simply 'cosmetic'.

FLAVOURINGS

These are used to strengthen the flavour of a product containing natural foods, or to simulate the taste of natural foods in non-natural products.

Number of different flavourings available 1900–2000:

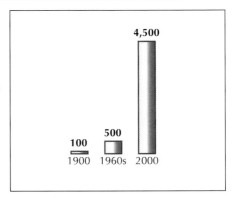

SWEETENERS

Excluding sugar, there are 13 other chemical compounds which are used as artificial sweeteners. One such sweetener, aspartame, provides virtually no calories.

Use of aspartame 1982–2000 worldwide in tonnes:

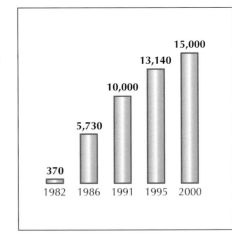

SAVOURY AND SWEET FOOD PRODUCTS

Savoury and sweet food products are usually found on separate shelves in shops, and are usually served as different courses during a meal. But strangely, many of these products contain similar basic ingredients – their sweet or savoury character is created by flavourings.

Colourings are used to modify the colour of a product. There are 40 different compounds available to the food industry, and they are used particularly in cereals, snack foods, desserts, sweets and drinks.

Preservatives are added to food to stop the growth of harmful bacteria, and there are 50 different compounds available. The most common are sulphur dioxide, sodium nitrate and potassium nitrate.

Flavour enhancers are chemicals which trick the eater into thinking that a food product has more flavour than it really does. The most common compound is MSG (monosodium glutamate), which is widely used in savoury products. About 650,000 tonnes of MSG are added to the world's food supply each year. 36 different flavour enhancer compounds are available to the food industry.

Emulsifiers and stabilisers are used to make sure that water and oil stay mixed together, and are particularly used in margarine and mayonnaise. Up to 75 different compounds are available.

Source: Extract from *The Atlas of Food*, by Erik Millstone and Tim Lang (Earthscan, 2003) Copyright © Myriad Editions/ www.MyriadEditions.com2003

1 List **four** effects of using chemical additives in food products. **[1]**

2 What do flavourings do to non-natural foods? **[1]**

3 How many tonnes of aspartame were added to food products in 2000? **[1]**

4 What is unusual about the content of many sweet and savoury products? **[1]**

5 Which type of additive can stop the growth of dangerous germs? **[1]**

6 What effect does MSG have? **[1]**

7 What are the additives used in margarine and mayonnaise for? **[1]**

8 Which additive is available in the highest number of chemical compounds? **[1]**

[Total: 8]

Exam exercise 2

Read the following internet article about eco-tourism in Argentina, and then answer the questions.

Establecimiento La Alegría is a wonderful new vacation spot immersed in the heart of the Argentine subtropical Paranaense rainforest. Situated in the northeast province of Misiones, within a multipurpose reserve, La Alegría covers an area of 30,000 hectares. This is the major biodiversity region of the country, with large rivers, clear streams and waterfalls, red soil and bright green jungle, full of giant and ancient trees, peculiar endemic flora and a large presence of wild fauna. There are more than 100 different species of trees, more than 2,000 identified plant species, and more than 400 species of birds, mammals and reptiles.

Because *Establecimiento La Alegría* sits on privately owned land, our guests are far from other tourists. Never crowded, our groups range from couples and honeymooners to larger groups of family and friends travelling together. Young and old alike are welcome.

With your own private group of friends, you may take as much or as little time as you like for those precious photographs. There is no need to rush to keep up with the group, because you *are* the group! You set your own pace and do exactly as you wish. Whether relaxing by the pool, reading under the shade of an ancient araucaria tree, or enjoying an evening drink followed by a night walk back to your accommodation in the lodge, every day is at *your* pace with a totally natural and unique style.

We are thrilled to invite you to experience this extraordinary place and enjoy our different eco-adventure programmes in a completely original and authentic style. For more information, please feel free to contact your local travel agent or us directly.

Geographic location

Argentine Republic, Province of Misiones, San Pedros municipality, kilometre No. 80 of the province route No. 17, coordinates S 26°26.617' latitude W053°58.394' longitude.

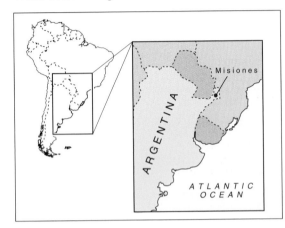

Getting there

Establecimiento La Alegría can be reached by plane, departing from Buenos Aires' Jorge Newbery airport to Posadas or Puerto Iguazu airports. Then, the travel agent transfers the visitors by road in a four-wheel drive vehicle or in a small rented aeroplane* to the lodge, where we take care of the traveller.

The best option and, at the same time, the most economical is for passengers to arrive at Puerto Iguazu airport, as it is only a few kilometres from *La Alegría*, while from Posadas airport, the *Eco Adventure Lodge* is more than 250 kilometres away.

(*) Aeroplanes: Cessna 172 XP Skyhawk (LV-OOU) and/or Cessna 182 RG Skylane (LV-OEM).

Activities

We offer custom-designed eco-adventures from this intimate and wonderful lodge: you can go horseriding, hiking, trekking or mountain biking through the wilderness. If you are feeling less energetic, why not try observing wildlife, walking photo safaris, discovering forest waterfalls, experiencing four-wheel drive vehicles in the jungle, exploring local villages, relaxing, strolling through gardens, and eating homemade delights in the main lodge or sipping delicious Argentine drinks as you watch the sun go down?

In *Establecimiento La Alegría* the guests are hosted by us, the owners. We welcome guests into our lodge as if they were members of our own family. Dining at *La Alegría* in an intimate atmosphere, we join our guests for a superb sit-down casual dinner every night. The cuisine is garden fresh, often grown on the premises, and the food is a combination of fine European cuisine and creative homestyle cooking. Dishes contain fresh meats and fish, and delicious desserts.

Accommodation

The wooden lodges provide beautiful and comfortable accommodation with rustic details: an entrance porch leading to a sitting area, a living room, bedrooms and a bathroom, with shower and bath. During winter, wood stoves provide heating. For light, at night a generator provides electricity and when turned off, kerosene lamps are used.

One of the lodges has 4 bedrooms (2 people per room), a living room, a dining room, a bathroom and a kitchen. The other lodge has space for 5 people and has 2 bedrooms (3 + 2), a living/dining room, a bathroom and a kitchen.

The *Establecimiento La Alegría* has a solarium decorated with plants, orchids and palms of the rainforest. The water in the swimming pool comes from a nearby water source. It is fresh and runs 24 hours a day, 365 days a year.

Source: Adapted from http://www.laalegrialodge.com.ar/English/index.htm, November 2003

1	What is the size of *La Alegría*?	[1]
2	Give **three** geographical features of the area.	[1]
3	Supply **three** pieces of evidence to show that the area has a wide variety of plants and animals.	[1]
4	What type of people stay at *Establecimiento La Alegría*?	[1]
5	How do visitors to *La Alegría* avoid being part of an organised group?	[1]
6	Give **two** ways in which more details can be obtained.	[1]
7	Which **two** methods of transport can be used to reach *Establecimiento La Alegría*?	[1]

8 What is the disadvantage in arriving at Posadas airport?   [1]

9 What activities are offered for people who do not feel very energetic?
   List **six**.   [2]

10 How is the accommodation heated during the colder months?   [1]

11 In what **two** ways is light provided?   [2]

12 How many people can stay in the two lodges at the same time?   [1]

[Total: 14]

Exam exercise 3

Read the following information and then complete the notes on page 150.

MÖBIUS AND THE RECYCLING LOGO

It is difficult to miss the triangle of three bent arrows that represents recycling. It appears in newspapers and magazines and on bottles, cans, envelopes, cardboard boxes and other containers.

But have you noticed that there are two versions of the recycling symbol? The difference between them lies in the direction of the twist in one of the three arrows that make up the symbol.

Standard Symbol

A mathematics professor, Cliff Long, noticed that the arrows of the standard recycling symbol are twisted in such a way that if they were joined together in a continuous ribbon, they would form a Möbius band. A Möbius band has only one side and one edge. You can make a Möbius band by gluing together the two ends of a long strip of paper after giving one end half a twist. This curious object is named after the astronomer and mathematician August Ferdinand Möbius (1790–1868), a professor at the University of Leipzig, who published his discovery about one-sided surfaces in 1865.

One day, Professor Long noticed a second version of the recycling symbol. This new version aroused his interest, and he carefully compared it with the one that was already familiar to him. He discovered that the new symbol was based on a one-sided band formed by gluing together the two ends of a long strip of paper after giving one end three half twists instead of just one. This second symbol probably came about through human error, as the original recycling symbol was designed by a student, Gary Anderson, in a competition in 1970.

Alternative Symbol

Because of the simplicity and clarity of Anderson's design, the recycling symbol has become widely used all over the world, and is now as common as many international products. The symbol has been revised over the years, and there are now different versions to represent different aspects of recycling.

The version with the arrows within a circle means that the product contains a certain amount of recycled material:

white arrows + black circle = 100% recycled content in the product

black arrows + white circle = a % of recycled content in the product

outline arrows + no circle = the product itself can be recycled

Möbius Band

But the science behind the Möbius phenomenon has practical applications as well. Take a look at the belt that drives a car's radiator fan. Ordinarily, friction wears the belt out more quickly on the inside than the outside. But when the belt is made with a half twist, like the Möbius strip, it has only one side and wears out more evenly and slowly.

Alternative Symbol

Source: Adapted from: http://www.sciencenews.org/20030426/mathtrek.asp 21/11/03 and http://www.mcmua.com/solidwaste/CreatingtheRecyclingSymbol.htm, November 2003

Examples of where recycling symbol used (**1**) ......

Difference between two versions is that (**2**) ......

Standard symbol similar to (**3**) ...... which has (**4**) ...... and (**5**) ...... and is named after (**6**) ......

Second symbol probably result of (**7**) ......

Different versions used for (**8**) ......

Practical application of Möbius (**9**) ......

Exam Exercise 4

Read the following article about a mission to Mars, and then complete the notes.

Mission to Mars

A new golden age in Mars exploration has begun. A host of space probes are leaving Earth for the Red Planet. First off was Europe's first solo mission to another planet, *Mars Express*. On board the parent spacecraft is *Beagle 2*, a tiny space-lander the size of a barbecue. If all goes well, it will become the first British-built probe to touch down on another world.

The whole mission cost £200m (€300m). The aim is simple: to find evidence of life, past or present, on another planet.

Mars Express

Mars Express is the European Space Agency's first planetary mission. It carries seven scientific instruments that will study the geology of the planet and search for water under the Martian surface. Research institutes throughout Europe have provided the instruments; the spacecraft was built by a consortium of 24 companies from 15 European countries and the USA.

The spacecraft will fly around Mars for an entire Martian year. Scientists are confident that if water is present on the Red Planet, *Mars Express* will find it.

Beagle 2

Beagle 2 will be the first space-lander to look specifically for evidence of life since the two Mars *Viking* probes of the 1970s. On landing, cameras on *Beagle*'s robotic arm will take close-up images of soil and rocks to look for interesting specimens. A drill on the robotic arm will collect samples from within rocks while a 'mole' will crawl slowly across the surface and grab soil from beneath boulders. The samples will be analysed for chemical signs of life using a package of instruments on the lander.

The launch

Mars Express, carrying the *Beagle 2* lander, was launched successfully from the Baikonur Cosmodrome in Kazakhstan on a Soyuz rocket. About 90 minutes into the flight, *Mars Express* was placed in the correct trajectory for its interplanetary voyage. The solar arrays opened and the spacecraft made contact with the ESA's ground station in Western Australia. If all goes well, the 400 million km journey to Mars will take just over six months.

Arrival

Mars Express will make preparations to drop *Beagle 2* by heading straight for the Red Planet. The lander will make a fiery plunge through the thin Martian atmosphere protected by a heat shield. As it nears the surface, parachutes will open to slow its descent. Just before touchdown, gas-filled bags will inflate to cushion the landing. *Beagle 2* should bounce to a halt on the Isidis basin, a flat, boulder-strewn plain. Meanwhile, *Mars Express* will fire its main engine and turn away from Mars ready to orbit the planet and begin the hunt for water.

Life search

There are tantalising clues that water once flowed on Mars. Pictures sent back by space probes show gullies and canyons that seem to have been carved by rivers and lakes. This water may now be trapped under the surface, possibly in huge quantities. *Mars Express* will search for this water using a ground-penetrating radar, known as MARSIS, that can probe up to 3,000 metres below the surface. If water exists, so too may life. Some scientists claim that rocks from Mars that have fallen to Earth contain evidence of primitive microbes.

Source: Adapted from: *http://news.bbc.co.uk/1/shared/spl/hi/sci_nat/03/race_to_mars/mission_guide/html/mars_express.stm*, November 2003

You are going to give a short talk about the mission to Mars to your class at school. Make **two** short notes under each heading below as a basis for your talk.

MISSION TO MARS

a   Cost and aim

b   Research equipment on *Beagle 2*

c   Landing on Mars

d   Water on Mars

Exam exercise 5

Read the following article about a new system to monitor the Amazon. Then write a summary outlining what the system will do. **You should write no more than 100 words.** You should use your own words as far as possible.

You will be given up to 6 marks for relevant points that you make and up to 4 marks for the way in which you write about these points.

Eye in the Sky

The Amazon, one of the world's remaining wilderness areas, is about to get a long-awaited aerial monitoring system to help protect the Brazilian rainforest system against illegal exploitation. The Brazilian Amazon covers 5.2 million square kilometres, and makes up more than 60% of Brazil's land area. It contains about a third of the world's remaining tropical rainforest, and about 30% of the world's biodiversity.

In the next few months, the $1.3bn Amazon surveillance system (Sivam) will be up and running, monitoring meteorological data and aerial activity over an area the size of Europe.

Twenty radar systems will be set up which will give the Brazilian Amazon complete coverage. The project, which is more than 95% ready, includes three surveillance aircraft, four satellite reception stations, 14 lightning detectors, 83 weather stations, 200 floating data-collection points and a network of 914 points linked by computer and fax. The integrated system will employ about 1,000 experts.

The new system will be able to catalogue and map Amazonian land better than before, and be able to detect forest fires and deforestation with more accuracy than the current methods. It will also be able to locate illegal airstrips with relative ease and see if people are invading land belonging to indigenous tribes.

The aim of harnessing the rainforest's resources has been a long-standing dream of successive Brazilian governments. In the late 1960s, the huge Trans-Amazon Highway was built, which only served to quicken deforestation, but Sivam will not be used for destructive purposes, according to experts. Also, while Brazil has borrowed the money to build Sivam, it hopes that it will end up saving the country money by cutting down on smuggling, forest fires and illegal mining.

Source: Adapted from an article by Alex Bellos, *The Guardian Weekly*, 18–24 October 2001

Exam exercise 6

DO YOU ENJOY DANCING?

Would you like to learn and perform dances from different countries?
Would you like to take part in workshops and dance in a theatre show?

If the answer is **YES**, then join the **MODERN DANCE SCHOOL**!

Write to us today for more information.

You have seen the leaflet above from the Modern Dance School.

Write a **letter** to the Modern Dance School in which you:

- describe yourself
- explain why you are interested in joining the Modern Dance School
- ask for more information

Your letter should be 150–200 words long (100–150 words for the Core curriculum).

You will receive up to 9 marks for the content of your writing, and up to 9 marks for the style and accuracy of your language (5 + 5 Core).

Exam exercise 7

Is the way people speak really important?

Write an article for your school magazine, giving your views on the importance of speaking correctly. You may use the comments below, but you are free to include your own ideas as well. Write between 150 and 200 words (100–150 for the Core curriculum).

You will receive up to 9 marks for the content of your writing, and up to 9 marks for the style and accuracy of your language (5 + 5 Core).

> We shouldn't judge people on the way they speak.
>
> People who speak correctly always get the best jobs.
>
> The way you speak says a lot about the person you are inside.
>
> TV and cinema have made us more aware of how we should speak.

Listening exam

Part 1
Questions 1–6

For questions 1–6 you will hear a series of short sentences. Answer each question as briefly as possible. You will hear each item twice.

1 Kerry has seen an advertisement for an office job and is telephoning the company.

    i   In what department does she hope to work?   **[1]**

    ii   When **exactly** are the interviews being held?   **[1]**

2 Jim and Mary are talking about television. Why does Jim think it's a good idea for them to buy a second TV?   **[1]**

3 Thandie is hoping to buy a theatre ticket at half the normal price for next Monday's performance. Why is it not possible to do so immediately?   **[1]**

4 You have arranged to drive to the seaside on Saturday. Why might it take you a long time to get there?   **[1]**

5 You have gone into town to buy some sports shoes but they are not available.

    i   How long will you have to wait before receiving them from this shop?   **[1]**

    ii   How might you be able to find some earlier than this?   **[1]**

6 Rachel and Richard have gone to a restaurant to have a celebration dinner. Why is the restaurant closed?   **[1]**

[Total: 8]

Part 2, Exercise 1

7 Listen to the following interview with Shanta Carlson, a marine biologist at the London Aquarium; then complete the notes below. You will hear the interview twice.

    a   Shanta starts work at around .... and normally finishes at ....   **[1]**

    b   Examples of maintenance to be done in the morning are:

       i   ....   **[1]**

       ii   ....   **[1]**

    c   When she is in the tanks with the sharks, she does not consider them to be dangerous because ....   **[1]**

    d   What she most dislikes about working on Monday morning is .... when cleaning the tanks.   **[1]**

    e   She might eventually work as a fish curator or ....   **[1]**

    f   What she thinks is the best aspect of her job: ....   **[1]**

[Total: 7]

Track 15

Part 2, Exercise 2

8   A school group is taking part in an activity holiday. The group leader is telling the students what they will be doing that week. Listen to what he says and then complete the Diary page. You will hear his speech twice.

Diary

<u>Monday</u>

      9.30 a.m.   Horseriding – specialist equipment supplied

a   Meet at .... **[1]**

b   8 p.m.   .... **[1]**

<u>Tuesday</u>

      a.m.   Selection of watersports

c   Check group details on .... **[1]**

      p.m.   Lecture about climbing practice and safety. Rock climbing.

<u>Wednesday</u>

d a.m.   Lesson on .... **[1]**

e p.m.   Hill walking. Bring .... **[1]**

<u>Thursday</u>

      a.m.   Choice of visits:

f   .... **[1]**

                historic house

                birdwatching at nature reserve

g p.m.   .... **[1]**

h Then .... and .... **[1]**

                                               [Total: 8]

Track 16

Part 3, Exercise 1

9 Listen to the following radio interview with a postman in the countryside; then answer the questions below. You will hear the interview twice.

   a Give **two** examples showing how involved Norman Dunbar becomes in the lives of the farmers. **[1]**

   b Why has he so far been successful in not losing his job? **[1]**

   c Describe the school he visits. **[1]**

   d Why does he sometimes get late on his rounds? **[1]**

   e When does he walk up steep slopes in thick snow? **[1]**

   f Why, according to him, are people in towns not quite so generous with their present-giving? **[1]**

[Total: 6]

Track 17

Part 3, Exercise 2

10 Listen to the interview about electricity on board aeroplanes; then answer the following questions. You will hear the interview twice.

   a How does an aircraft get its electrical power? **[1]**

   b How much electricity do 15 homes use? **[1]**

   c List **five** sources of electrical consumption on board an aircraft. **[2]**

   d What is the purpose of the emergency generator? **[1]**

   e List **two** ways in which an aircraft can obtain electrical power if it is parked in an airport. **[2]**

[Total: 7]

Appendix 1: Speaking test cards

In the Speaking test, your teacher/examiner will begin by asking you a few general questions about yourself/school/home, etc. This is not part of the examination – it is intended to put you at your ease!

After that you will be handed one test card and given a little time to think about the topic described on it. You will then have a conversation for a few minutes with your teacher/examiner based on the topic. Eight examples from past test cards are given below.

Memories of early childhood

Discuss with the Examiner some of the memories you have of the time when you were very young.

You may wish to consider such things as:

- your earliest memory
- the house you lived in and its surroundings
- your parents, brothers and sisters
- some events that you remember clearly
- your first days at school
- family holidays

You are free to discuss any other ideas of your own.

You are not allowed to make any written notes.

The clothes I like

Discuss with the Examiner the types of clothes you like wearing and the things that influence your choices.

You may wish to consider such things as:

- whether you follow the latest fashion
- what your parents think of what you wear
- whether there are any types of clothes that you would not wear
- the influence of famous people on your choices
- whether your friends' opinions are important
- whether clothes reveal the character of the wearer

You are free to consider any ideas of your own.

You are not allowed to make any written notes.

Changes in lifestyle

Discuss with the Examiner the changes that have occurred in the way people live in your country since the time that your grandparents were teenagers.

You may wish to consider such things as:

- standards of living; income and possessions
- standards of health care and knowledge about healthy living
- attitudes to religion and other beliefs
- the way that teenagers behave at home and at school
- the clothes that are worn by teenagers
- opportunities to travel and knowledge of the world

You are free to consider any ideas of your own.

You are not allowed to make any written notes.

Education as a preparation for work

Nearly everyone will one day have to earn a living by getting a job.

Discuss with the Examiner how the education you have had so far (and any further education or training you intend to take) will, in your opinion, prepare you for the world of work.

You may wish to consider:

- subjects you are studying which might help you in a job
- whether the study habits you have will be useful later on
- whether some of your subjects seem to have little to do with your intended career
- whether part-time work while you are still at school or college might be a good idea
- aspects of school life, apart from subjects you study, that help you when you work

You are free to discuss any ideas of your own.

You are not allowed to make any written notes.

! EXAM TIP

Remember, the topics are very general, and the Speaking test is *not* a test of your knowledge about a topic. Your teacher/examiner is interested in how you use English: your vocabulary and the structure of your sentences, for example.

Climate change

We are seeing more and more evidence that the weather in many parts of the world is changing – sometimes with disastrous results.

Discuss with the Examiner possible reasons for these changes and what steps might be taken to deal with the problem.

You may wish to consider such things as:

- what might be causing these changes in climate
- some examples of disasters caused by these changes
- steps taken in your country to guard against adverse weather conditions
- what might be done on a worldwide basis
- whether climate change might be an advantage in some parts of the world

You are free to consider any ideas of your own.

You are not allowed to make any written notes.

Things you enjoy at school

Most students find some aspects of their school lives enjoyable – other aspects less so.

Discuss with the Examiner your feelings about your life at school.

You may wish to consider:

- the subjects you find particularly enjoyable and why
- activities at school that you always look forward to
- aspects of school life that you find difficult
- sport and leisure activities that you take part in at school
- what you will miss most when you leave school

You are free to consider any ideas of your own.

You are not allowed to make any written notes.

Study abroad

Nowadays, many young people spend some time studying away from their home country.

Discuss with the Examiner some of the advantages of studying abroad and some of the difficulties young people might encounter if they do.

You may wish to consider:

- what you might learn from the experience of a different country
- how study abroad might be an advantage in higher education or employment
- some of the problems of living and learning in a foreign country
- difficulties of settling down after a period away from home
- possible difficulties of leaving your own country and culture

You are free to consider any ideas of your own.

You are not allowed to make any written notes.

Road accidents and road safety

There are more and more worries about the number of people who are injured in accidents on roads.

Discuss with the Examiner some of the causes of road accidents, and how roads could be made safer.

You may wish to consider such things as:

- why accidents happen
- who are most likely to have accidents – pedestrians, cyclists, motorists
- some consequences of road accidents
- some steps that might be taken to reduce the number of accidents
- how the laws in your country might be changed to reduce the number of accidents

You are free to consider any ideas of your own.

You are not allowed to make any written notes.

UNIT 4: Listening 1, Exercise 6

Speaker 1

Well, of course, we had booked everything well in advance, because in Britain these services get full very early, and we didn't want to be disappointed. Anyway, we got to the terminus in central London in plenty of time, and we stood on platform 13E for Edinburgh. It was a beautiful summer day. There was me, my wife Julia and the three children. They were still quite young then: 3, 6 and 8, I think. We were supposed to leave at 8.30 in the morning, and as it got closer to our departure time, we all began to get quite excited. By 8.30, we had started to get a little bit anxious because the platform was completely empty, apart from us five with all our luggage. At 9.00, Julia told me to go and find out what was happening, so off I went to the booking office to make enquiries. And yes, you can guess what was wrong – we were 12 hours early! Our departure time was 8.30 pm, not am. I had misread the time on the tickets.

Speaker 2

They call it an airport, but it's really just a field. My sister had booked me a flight as a treat for my twentieth birthday, which was May 20, three years ago, and I must admit that I was absolutely dreading it! I've never really enjoyed flying, and the thought of going up in the air for 30 minutes in a basket really didn't appeal to me. I couldn't understand how the thing was driven and steered, and I think that's what put me off. But once we got up in the air, at 9 o'clock in the morning, it was spectacular, the most beautiful views of the hills, fields and villages below, with the sun sparkling on the river. We didn't want to come down!

Speaker 3

I had investigated all the different options available to me, and in the end this was by far the cheapest at only $275. Of course, it wouldn't be nearly as fast as going by plane, but the cost was far less, and I would be able to see something of the countryside. Some friends had travelled the same route the previous year and had said how brilliant it had been, so I wasn't really worried. What they hadn't told me was how uncomfortable these vehicles are when you've been in one for almost two days. It's very difficult to sleep, and there are no toilets or washing facilities, so you've got to hang on until the scheduled stops, usually every four to five hours. When I finally arrived in the south of Spain, after nearly 48 hours on the road, I slept for over 19 hours!

Speaker 4

We set sail late for Belgium just as the sun was setting on the horizon. There was a horrible smell of petrol and diesel from all the cars, but the breeze soon blew away the fumes and I was able to stand outside on the deck for the whole journey, even though it was the middle of winter and the air was extremely cold. We moved quite slowly, but it was very relaxing. Quite often we saw lights travelling in the other direction, but apart from that, I felt totally alone, out there in the open, without a sound except for the distant hum of the engines and the spray falling around me.

UNIT 4: Listening 2, Exercise 29

Question 1   Marina calls her local college to get some information about evening classes. What course does Marina want to follow?

Marina: Hello. Could you send me information about your evening classes?

College: Of course. Are you interested in anything in particular, or do you want details of everything we offer?

Marina: I'd like to learn Italian.

Question 2   Gregory is telephoning a music store to order a CD. What is the order number?

Store: Good morning, Mega Music Store. Can I help you?

Gregory: Hello, I'd like to know if I can order the new Discovery CD.

Store: Certainly. Let me check on the computer *(pause)*. Yes, the order number is CD39 dash 2BK. The price is £13.99.

Gregory: Thank you very much.

Question 3   Jeremy is trying to arrange for his cousin Melanie to come to visit him. When is she **un**able to stay?

Jeremy: So, when do you think you can come and stay?

Melanie: Well, I'm free from the 11th to the 18th of this month, and also from the 22nd to the 29th, but the 19th until the 21st is impossible for me. I'll be away on a course.

Question 4   You are planning a day trip for tomorrow. What will the weather be like **throughout** the day? Give **two** aspects.

Radio: Here is the weather forecast for tomorrow for your local area. There will be sunny spells in the early morning, but it will cloud over by midday, with the possibility of heavy showers by late afternoon. A strong breeze will persist until the evening. The temperature will reach a maximum of 18 degrees Celsius.

Question 5   You and your friend play badminton at your local sports centre. How much does it cost to book a court on a weekday evening?

Speaker: Hi everyone. Just a few announcements to make before we all go home. The sports centre management has just introduced new prices for using the facilities, so from next week a badminton court will cost £6.90 per hour, which is an increase of 50 pence. However, as club members, we will be charged a reduced price of £5.80.

Question 6   Michael wants to go to an art exhibition which he has seen advertised in the newspaper and is asking someone for details. From where can he buy tickets?

Michael: Hello. I'd like some information about the art exhibition advertised in today's newspaper.

Info: Yes, of course. It opens this weekend, and continues until the end of the month. The exhibition is open to the public from 10 in the morning, and closes at 7 pm. Admission is only available with a ticket bought in advance. These are available from the venue booking office.

Michael: Thank you very much for your help.

UNIT 4: Listening 3, Exercise 32

Some of Britain's best-known tourist attractions, including Buckingham Palace and Canterbury Cathedral, have this week been described as overpriced, according to the new Consumers' Group *Guide to Attractions*. The guide covers more than 300 attractions, ranging from castles to zoos and from museums to theme parks. Canterbury Cathedral gets special criticism for its charge of £3.50 for a guided tour, while visitors to York Minster enjoy free entrance. Out of 20 attractions visited, eight received only one star out of five for quality, including Buckingham Palace. According to the guide, visitors will be severely disappointed if they hope to find out about the royal family by visiting the palace. However, Hampton Court, another royal palace, scores maximum marks for value for money, and is among the top ten attractions. The variety of standards has led to a demand by the Consumers' Group for a national grading system to be introduced. But its demands are fiercely opposed by the tourism industry, which claims such comparisons are meaningless. The editor of the guide, Jane Ingman, singled out Buckingham Palace as the attraction she likes least. She complains that the palace simply takes people's money and gives nothing in return. The guide, which is published by the Consumers' Group, is available from all good bookshops. Happy reading!

UNIT 9: Listening 1, Exercise 5

Pablo Selles: We are very lucky to have in our studio today Janine Mesumo, who works as a careers advisor at an international school in Madrid. Her main role is to advise students who have recently completed their IGCSEs, AS and A levels on what they should do next. Part of this is giving them advice on writing their first CV. Have I got that right, Janine?

Janine Mesumo: Absolutely, Pablo. Actually, a great deal of my time is spent in helping students draw up their CV, which can be quite problematic when you haven't yet had any work experience.

PS: What areas should first-time CV writers include?

JM: I think the key here is not to try to include too much. Prospective employers need to be able to get a quick overview, rather than a detailed biography of someone's life – that can come at the interview. However, there needs to be enough information so that the employer can decide whether or not to call the applicant for an interview.

PS: Hmm, I see. So what information would you say is essential?

JM: Start with personal details: name, address, contact details. You'd be surprised how many people forget to put their telephone number and address on their CV! Then, education and qualifications. Some people recommend combining these two areas, so, for example, you might say '1999–2001, International School, Madrid, six IGCSEs in Maths, English', and so on, rather than listing the qualifications in a different section.

PS: That's an interesting idea, I like that! What comes next?

JM: Well, this is where some students become rather worried, because usually the next section is work experience.

PS: But often students don't have any work experience!

JM: Exactly, and so they worry about leaving a blank. But as a school-leaver, nobody is going to expect you to have an employment history, so there really is no need to worry. However, it is worth mentioning weekend or after-school jobs, or any work for charities, or voluntary work.

PS: OK, and after that? What about hobbies and interests?

JM: Yes, it is important to include leisure interests, but a common mistake is simply to list things, for example: reading, football, music.

PS: So what should our listeners do?

JM: Instead of simply giving a list, explain in what way these things interest you. For example, if you put reading, give details about what you like to read …

PS: … and if you list music, what type of music you like listening to.

JM: Exactly, but also, music might mean playing an instrument, so give that information as well.

PS: Any other sections which need to be included?

JM: Well, two really. The first should include any skills which have not been mentioned before, such as proficiency in other languages (don't just put 'French'!), and details of any organisations or clubs which you belong to. And finally, give the names, addresses and contact details for two referees.

PS: Which are what?

JM: A referee is a person who would be willing to write about you in a positive way! Always check with the person before you put their name on your CV.

PS: Janine, we're coming to the end of our time. Thank you very much for a very informative chat. If any listeners would like more information about writing their CV, we have a special leaflet …

UNIT 9: Listening 2, Exercise 13

Interviewer: Good morning, Mr Gennaro, please take a seat.

Interviewee: Thanks.

Int'er: Did you have any problems getting here?

Int'ee: Nope, I found the address very easily cos I checked it out yesterday.

Int'er: I see … now, you've just left school with four IGCSEs, is that correct?

Int'ee: Yeah.

Int'er: And the subjects?

Int'ee: Oh, right, err, let me think now … science, English, art and music.

Int'er: Thank you. Which of those was your favourite subject at school?

Int'ee: I didn't really like any of them. The teachers were not very interesting. I must've been really lucky to pass them.

Int'er: And which school did you attend?

Int'ee: The new one, behind the park at the start of the motorway.

Int'er: I see. Now, tell me something about your interests, the things that you do in your free time.

Int'ee: Well, I like going to discos, and music, and riding my bike. That's why I think this job would be good for me.

Int'er: Because you like riding a bike?

Int'ee: Er, yeah. The job's to do with sport, innit?

Int'er: Yes, Mr Gennaro, it is. Have you had any work experience yet, for example a weekend job?

Int'ee: Well, yeah, I had a job with my brother washing cars in our street. We used to do it in our free time and I was like, wicked! We got loads of money to spend on clothes and CDs, or for going to the cinema and discos.

Int'er: What personal qualities do you think you could offer us here at Winning Sports?

Int'ee: Well, like I told you, I like sports, especially riding my bike, and every weekend I go to the match, if they're playing at home of course. What else do you want to know?

Int'er: I think that's all for the time being, Mr Gennaro.

Int'ee: Is that it?

Int'er: Yes, thank you very much, Mr Gennaro. That's all. Goodbye.

Int'ee: Did I get the job?

Int'er: I'll be in touch. Goodbye.

UNIT 14: Listening 1, Exercise 6

Florence Nightingale was born in Italy on the 12th May 1820 and was named Florence after her birthplace. Her parents, Fanny and William, were wealthy and spent a considerable amount of time touring Europe. As a schoolchild, Florence was academic, and rarely had problems with her studies. She was attractive, and the expectation was that she would marry and start a family.

However, Florence had different ideas. As a teenager she became involved in the social questions of the day, making visits to homes for sick people in local villages, and began to investigate hospitals and nursing. Her parents refused to allow her to become a nurse, as in the mid nineteenth century it was not considered a suitable profession for a well-educated woman. Because of the conflict which arose between Florence and her parents, it was decided to send her to Europe with some family friends, Charles and Selina Bracebridge.

The three travelled to Italy, Greece and Egypt, returning to England through Germany in July 1850. While in Germany, they visited a hospital near Dusseldorf, where Florence returned in the following year to undergo a three-month nurse training course. This enabled her to take a post at a clinic in London in 1853.

In March 1854, Britain was at war with Russia. While the Russians were defeated in the autumn of that year, British newspapers criticised the medical facilities for the soldiers wounded during the fighting. In response to the criticism, the government appointed Florence Nightingale to oversee the introduction of female nurses into British military hospitals in Turkey, and on the 4th November 1854, she arrived in Scutari with a group of 38 nurses. Initially, the doctors did not want the nurses there because they felt threatened, but within 10 days many more casualties arrived and all the nurses were needed to cope with this sudden influx of wounded soldiers.

The introduction of female nurses in military hospitals was an outstanding success, and the nation showed its gratitude to Florence Nightingale by honouring her with a medal in 1907. Throughout her life she continued tirelessly to campaign for better conditions in hospitals, and for improved health standards. When she died on the 13th August 1910, having been a complete invalid herself and totally blind for 15 years, she was a national heroine. Her farsighted reforms have influenced the nature of modern health care and her writings continue to be a resource for nurses, health managers and planners.

UNIT 14: Listening 2, Exercise 20

(Note that ICRC stands for International Committee of the Red Cross/Crescent)

Marianna Milutinovic: Today we welcome Alvaro Solomou, one of the 1,200 relief workers with the Red Cross, the ICRC, who is going to talk to us about the ICRC's approach to giving assistance. Welcome to the programme, Alvaro.

Alvaro Solomou: Hello, Marianna, and thank you for inviting me.

MM: Alvaro, can you tell us about how the ICRC assists victims of famine and drought, and other natural disasters?

AS: Well, we should remember that all too often natural disasters happen in areas where there is already some other sort of problem, such as an economic crisis, or a period of political instability. Put the two together, and the people involved become even more insecure and desperate.

MM: I imagine that different contexts also create extra problems, don't they?

AS: Yes, geographic context, as well as ethnic, political and economic, all translate into different needs and therefore the response the ICRC makes must be adapted to suit the context.

MM: How is that done?

AS: We use what is called the 'Assistance Pyramid'. This establishes that preference must be given in any relief situation to the foundations of the pyramid, in other words, to food, water, and essential goods, before anything else is done.

MM: What about health care? Isn't that a priority?

AS: Hygiene and medical care take second and third places in the pyramid. Obviously, if a person is starving and thirsty, it does not matter how good the health care is.

MM: I see. Does the ICRC only assist when there is a crisis?

AS: No, not at all. In fact, in recent years it has been the policy to provide help in developing countries once a crisis has passed, or even before one has occurred.

MM: How is that actually done?

AS: Well, for example, the ICRC assistance programmes have been extended so that they now include seed and tools distribution, and the provision of veterinary care. The ICRC identifies priorities in a region in order to provide the best possible assistance.

MM: Going back to the issue of water for a moment, isn't it true that millions of people across the world have difficulties gaining access to water? What can the ICRC do about this?

AS: Oh yes, that's absolutely true, and of course in many places the water that is available is actually extremely unhealthy, and may carry waterborne diseases such as cholera and typhoid. The ICRC has a programme of assistance which includes construction, engineering and providing access to water, along with hygiene and environmental protection, thus ensuring that water is clean and safe to use.

MM: Is it dangerous working for the ICRC?

AS: Well, in any crisis situation there are dangers, but all of us are strongly motivated by humanitarian work, and hopefully we can all cope with stress and the pressures which are bound to exist.

MM: Alvaro, thank you for giving us such an interesting insight into the work of the ICRC.

UNIT 19: Listening 1, Exercise 9

Interviewer: Hello and welcome to this week's edition of 'Technology Tomorrow'. Our guest today is Giovanni Conte, who was last year voted most influential designer of the 90s. Hello, Giovanni.

Giovanni
Conte: Hello.

Int: Giovanni, is it true that the clothes industry is technically backward?

GC: Absolutely! Although the actual fibres have changed considerably over the centuries, the clothes-making process is the same: spin the fibre into thread, weave the thread into cloth, cut it into pieces, and then sew it back together again to make an item of clothing. Very simple, really.

Int: But I understand all this is about to change, isn't it?

GC: Yes, and it's incredibly exciting. I have got together with GHK Electrics and The Jeane Company to produce a range of technical clothing. We have incorporated GHK mobile phone and MP3 technology into a range of jackets designed by me and made by The Jeane Company.

Int: Mobile phones and MP3 technology incorporated into clothes? How?

GC: The jackets, which will soon be available in the shops, feature phones which can be dialled using voice recognition technology, and a microphone and earphones built into the hood or collar. The MP3 player automatically cuts out when the phone rings, like on an aircraft when an announcement is made. Everything is controlled via a keypad hidden beneath a pocket flap.

Int: What happens when it gets dirty?

GC: The whole range is machine-washable.

Int: Where do you get your design ideas from?

GC: Over the years I have collected clothes from all over the world, and in my studio in Bologna I have built up a wardrobe of more than 50,000 garments, mostly military uniforms, which provide me with inspiration for my designs.

Int: Apart from the phone and MP3 player, what else could be incorporated into your designs?

GC: Currently I am looking at the possibility of building in a face-recognition camera, which would provide you with information about a person when you meet them again. Parents could keep an eye on their children through miniature cameras. And all this technology will be invisible, submerged in the fabric. It won't be long before all clothes contain some sort of micro-computer.

Int: But with all this in-built technology, will clothes still look fashionable?

GC: Of course, it's very important that clothes look beautiful, so I have tried to achieve the right balance between fashion and usefulness, just as The Jeane Company first did in 1874. My designs do not look like clothes from space!

Int: Giovanni, thank you very much for an extremely interesting look at what we'll all be wearing next year!

UNIT 19: Listening 2, Exercise 18

When shoes are made to fit your feet and nobody else's, they are called bespoke shoes. Bespoke shoes say something about you, not least that you are fairly wealthy and can afford to spend about £1,500 on a pair of shoes. Bespoke shoes are like buying a Ferrari car to drive around in, or a Gucci handbag to keep your credit cards in. Bespoke shoes make a statement.

There are now only five companies in London which still make traditional bespoke men's shoes. Surprisingly, bespoke shoes for women are made in Paris. The premises for these London companies are small, dark and cramped, full of antique-looking tools and rolls of leather, and with a smell that can only mean one thing: not twenty-first century.

Bespoke shoes are made in exactly the same way as they were one hundred years ago as the technology is completely unchanged. It still takes three months to make the first pair of shoes for a client, who must come in for at least three fittings. It is a process of customising, of gradual building. Along with the shoe, one thing that is being built is the ego of the client.

The process is as follows: you put your foot on a sheet of paper, called a 'book', and the shoemaker draws a line around it. Four measurements are taken: heel to toe, the width at the widest point, around the instep, and instep to heel. This is the first fitting. Next, a wooden model of your foot is made, called a 'last'. Then, the leather work begins.

The designs, like the process, have remained unchanged for a century. It is not that new fashions could not be introduced, it is simply that the clients do not want them. They want their shoes to be as they were one hundred years ago. The idea of a platform heel, a multicoloured shoe, or a trainer is unknown to the maker of the bespoke shoe and the client.